KU-436-100

Leslie E. Sheldon (ed.)

DIRECTIONS FOR THE FUTURE

Issues in English for Academic Purposes

PETER LANG

Oxford · Bern · Berlin · Bruxelles · Frankfurt am Main · New York · Wien

KING ALFRED'S COLLEGE
LIBRARY

Bibliographic information published by Die Deutsche Bibliothek
Die Deutsche Bibliothek lists this publication in the Deutsche
Nationalbibliografie; detailed bibliographic data is available on the
Internet at ‹http://dnb.ddb.de›.

British Library and Library of Congress Cataloguing-in-Publication
Data: A catalogue record for this book is available from The British
Library, Great Britain, and from The Library of Congress, USA

KING ALFRED'S COLLEGE
WINCHESTER

02869322 428
LAN

Cover design: Thomas Jaberg, Peter Lang AG

ISBN 3-03910-059-9
US-ISBN 0-8204-6875-4

© Peter Lang AG, European Academic Publishers, Bern 2004
Hochfeldstrasse 32, Postfach 746, CH-3000 Bern 9, Switzerland
info@peterlang.com, www.peterlang.com, www.peterlang.net

All rights reserved.
All parts of this publication are protected by copyright.
Any utilisation outside the strict limits of the copyright law, without
the permission of the publisher, is forbidden and liable to prosecution.
This applies in particular to reproductions, translations, microfilming,
and storage and processing in electronic retrieval systems.

Printed in Germany

DIRECTIONS FOR THE FUTURE

WITHDRAWN FROM
THE LIBRARY

UNIVERSITY OF
WINCHESTER

KA 0286932 2

Dedicated to my wife Terry, whose enthusiasm and creativity were central to the success of the BALEAP 2001 conference.

Contents

Section 4: Writing for Academic Purposes

Section 5: Testing and Evaluation

Section 6: Research and Publication

Introduction

One particularly interesting aspect of the 2001 conference of the British Association of Lecturers in English for Academic Purposes (EAP) held at the University of Strathclyde in Glasgow, Scotland, was that so many practitioners, from the UK and around the world, wanted to discuss concrete issues relating to what might at first sight be construed as 'traditional' concerns and issues: essay writing, the future of EAP (as a support activity within, but not always part of, the institutional mainstream), the best pedagogical approaches to use with Chinese learners, curriculum design, the effectiveness of tutorials/ EAP courses, critical thinking (as a strategy helpful for EAP learners in their reading/writing), and the role of research and publication within the profession. The emphasis appeared to be on practicalities, the focus still on making sure that, even in this Age of New Technology, all students are given help with the 'paper' study and research skills which still command institutional respect, and which have always comprised our professional targets as teachers.

Section 1 of this volume deals with the challenges – and possibilities – facing EAP in the first decades of this new century. Tony Dudley-Evans celebrates the characteristic eclectic, practical, and international focus of EAP. We must balance pedagogical pragmatism by research, however, and a key part of Dudley-Evans' focus is on the need to find out more about the increasing emergence of the EAP practitioner as a 'rights analyst'. The teacher does not only discover the technicalities of the academic tasks a student faces at the institutional level. Rather, in a change from the standard EAP paradigm, he or she should empower learners to request clarification of their lecturers in an active manner and, where appropriate, even challenge them.

For Dudley-Evans an equally important matter is the issue of specificity in EAP, and he observes that genre analysis has given more support to the idea that different academic fields have their distinctive purposes, genres, epistemology, and mechanisms for the reporting of knowledge claims. With this in mind the suggestion that a single academic writing course, for example, could be expected to provide effective help for students across a wide range of subject areas is perhaps suspect.

Ron White considers the future of the profession by examining realities which university EAP units face: they are often non-mainstream, being excluded from the communication and command structures of their respective institutions, frequently by virtue of their 'self-funding' ethos. The vulnerability inherent in such potential isolation is worsened by the increasing competitiveness of private language schools in the EAP arena. On the positive side, however, institutional EAP centres are potentially able to undertake funded pedagogic research in pan-departmental contexts, particularly with regard to the teaching impacts of new technology. In the coming years EAP centres could carve out a role for themselves as foci of in-novation, while helping to establish EAP as a significant field in its own right.

Section 2 concerns the cognitive enablement of EAP learners through explicit training in, for example, recognising the use of conceptual metaphors by subject lecturers, and in critical thinking (arriving at reason-based judgement through reflection, objective evaluation and the effective communication of these judgements). Jeanette Littlemore describes a study wherein cognitive instruction was provided in order to develop the critical academic reading abilities of international students, encouraging them to recognise the metaphors which underscore discussions of theoretical concepts and to appreciate their function in helping writers to structure their arguments.

Ros Richards explores critical thinking with specific regard to student writing, basing her discussion on a target model which includes a melding of such factors as linguistic proficiency, rhetorical awareness, and a proactive, putatively 'Western' approach to enquiry (including reflection, criticism, and analysis). Commenting in the main on students having a Confucian cultural heritage, she advocates the explicit teaching of metacognitive strategies which encourage learners both to discern how academic text is structured and to make use of these in their own writing.

The expectations and cultural values of EAP learners are described in Section 3, with David Catterick outlining a study aimed at identifying a 'belief inventory' relevant to Chinese students (an increasing EAP student constituency). The beliefs of many such students were found to be significantly at odds with those of British English Language Teaching (ELT) instructors, for example, an outcome which Catterick feels could be dealt with in a number of ways, including the outright alteration of learners' beliefs through explicit learner training in the values of the host institution. Andy Curtis, outlining the Effective English for Postgraduate Research Students programme at the Hong Kong Polytechnic University, likewise emphasises the importance of identifying learner needs rather than taking anything for granted, particularly in uncovering the graduate/undergraduate and discipline-specific factors that can influence the design of effective EAP support courses. Fiona Cotton also explores the frequent divergence between learner/teacher values, and makes the point that the differences in instructor/learner perspectives are greater than is often appreciated, the intuition of 'Western' EAP lecturers not always producing an accurate picture of what students expect with regard to such factors as teacher/student roles and responsibilities.

As Martha Jones and Roger Bird note, corpus linguistics and discourse analysis are tools which can be successfully applied to the spoken English actually used in both academic and general communication contexts with the objective of designing appropriate teaching materials whose objective it is to make students aware of the linguistic features of lectures, seminars, and casual conversations. In the sampling the authors describe, linkages were observed between particular language items and such communicatively functional characteristics as interactiveness and shared context. Making use of Wmatrix (an electronic corpus tool which provides retrieval and statistical functions, as well as concordancing), it was determined that the highest lexical density was found in casual conversation rather than lectures, suggesting academic discourse is less 'fact-based' or 'content-stacked' than one might intuitively assume. The emphasis here, as well as in many other articles in the collection, is the need to determine the characteristics of *actual* language use, with a view to making EAP pedagogy more effective.

With respect to learning styles, Zoe Kantaridou maintains that the development of student autonomy must be gradual and done with a sensitive understanding of learners' educational preferences. On the basis of an in-house analysis in Greece of what students feel are the characteristics of an ideal classroom context, there would seem to be a view that the teacher is central to the educational experience; he/she must communicate effectively with students, demonstrate an obvious, motivating love of his/her job and, perhaps not surprisingly, be able to use new technologies in order to make learning more interesting. Kantaridou makes the point that the results of such a belief survey can have a concrete effect on actual course design, and she describes a programme wherein students are increasingly encouraged to take the helm and become stakeholders, by identifying their linguistic goals, finding alternative sources of information/reference (in part by using the Internet), and studying on their own. Only a slow, bottom-up weaning of students from their preconceptions of teacher-centrality can cause them to adopt more independent learning modes.

The need to appreciate what is actually happening in the institutional 'real world' is a theme continued by John Straker in his consideration of how students, tutors, and other departments view EAP tutorials, which he feels really reflect the generally low status of EAP within the university mainstream. On the basis of a learner and tutor belief survey, the author maintains the instructors themselves were often more cynical about the value of the EAP tutorial than students, frequently believing they were operating as little more than a 'correction service'. EAP practitioners today have various interdepartmental respect issues, which affect their perceptions of job status and role in their institutions.

Most institutions see the improvement of student writing as central to EAP programmes, and the theory is that during the process of remediation knowledgeable, communicatively-inclined instructors are able to wean their students away from an inordinate concern for bottom-up matters (e.g., spelling, punctuation, and grammar), and more towards an awareness of textual features (e.g., discourse structure, rhetorical markers). As revealed by the case studies described in Section 4, however, actual experience suggests that this is not always the situation, and that instructors must be careful not to make such idealistic assumptions.

As Anderson, Benson, and Lynch note, the provision of feedback to students about their writing is seen as essential, though in the institutional context described, the actual interaction/timing of such feedback (and exactly what use students make of it) reveals a possible gap between stated expectations and practical performance. A majority of students indicated that it was important for them to minimise errors, and that they preferred teachers to locate an error and perhaps give a 'clue', rather than supplying the correct form; they also maintained that they looked more carefully at marks relating to discourse structure rather than grammar or vocabulary. Despite this apparent constructivist stance on the part of learners, the authors' study of teacher/student tutorial interaction revealed there was in fact more emphasis on lexicogrammatical items than higher order textual concerns, and that there is a seeming mismatch between what EAP institutions identify as their priorities, and what teachers actually provide and what students want much of the time.

Johnson Kalu reminds us it is essential to assess rigorously the productivity/effectiveness of an institution's EAP writing courses, to ensure the ultimate career and personal needs of one's student constituencies are met. In the context of the University of Botswana, the putative aim is to cater to the English language needs of students in order for them to function within the university itself, and in numerous professional target communities outside academia, but his data reveal there is still a tension between the need to develop critical literacy and independent learning and the power of the *status quo* (which emphasises rote learning and an inadequate awareness of what constitutes plagiarism) still preferred by many students. There is a need not only to review the nature of the programmes being offered with a view to making them more meaningful, but to realise that what happens in the EAP course is also affected by the writing expectations in the specialist disciplines themselves. Task-based, constructivist, text-level EAP tuition can have little impact unless the target con-stituencies themselves value the particular literacies being practised. In such a context, EAP can be a harbinger of new ideas for other departments.

One tends on the basis of experience and traditional expectation to equate EAP constituencies with international (i.e., non-native speakers of English) rather than 'home' students. As Siân Preece reminds us, in twenty-first century Britain this demarcation does not hold true any longer; referring to the situation at the University of Westminster, she notes that bilingual learners who have been educated in the United Kingdom are on the increase – a development which suggests traditional EAP pedagogies and foci may not have all the answers. The matter involves complex issues of language expertise, affiliation, and inheritance which need to be taken into account; such 'code switching' learners (who alternate between English and another language they speak within their cultural group) are not easily catered for by standard EAP provisions. Cultural 'hybridity' means such learners have a composite British/non-British (and even anti-British) identity, reflected in their linguistic choices; they may, for example, be reluctant to adopt formal English registers, even though these are typical EAP pedagogical targets. (In fact, it is felt that only a minority of British school students are habitual speakers of standard English and that a gravitation towards non-standard English is the norm.) Helping such students to become part of academic discourse communities, while respecting their multicultural UK identities and language choices represents a new challenge for EAP in the first decades of the new century.

In keeping with the emphasis in this volume on the interplay between theory and practice (and the need to find out more about actual language student language use), Section 5 deals with matters of testing and evaluation, from the perspective of a particular in-stitutional context and, on a much larger scale, the revision of the International English Language Testing System (IELTS) speak-ing test.

Alan Tonkyn and Julia Wilson describe the formal revision process, which was particularly informed by the realities of language performance as these have been discovered by linguistics researchers. In the assessment context, for example, it has been determined that at lower proficiency levels grammatical features seem to be central to scores awarded, whereas at higher levels, discoursal features play a larger role. In the light also of collective IELTS examiner experience, the revision involved the replacement of the previous holistic scale with a more focused analytical scale isolating such features at fluency and coherence and lexical resource. The new speaking test evinces a closer specification of examiner linguistic interaction with candidates by means of an examiner script (called a 'frame'), which ensures all assessors use consistent phraseology and avoid excessive 'examiner-talk'. The provision of a new 'long turn' task which produces pro-longed testee spoken discourse (speaking coherently on a discussion topic, using prompts written on a card), has been provided to ensure examiners are provided with assessable candidate output.

On the other hand, Turner, Godwin, and Wilks describe the use of a bespoke vocabulary profiling program called PLex, which analyses the difficulty of spoken discourse on the basis of monitoring the occurrence of low frequency, academically 'formal' vocabulary items. An examination of transcribed conversational tasks at the University of Wales indicated the improvement of EAP students was not evinced through an increasing use of 'hard' words – as one might expect – but via gauging the students' more general ability to adapt their spoken registers to the exigencies of particular communicative situations. Indeed, it is felt that the kind of general topics often used in English lessons and formal EAP examinations may not elicit the level of vocabulary sophistication/use which is often considered an indication of enhanced proficiency; moreover, the evidence appears to show that tutor 'intuition' about whether particular words were 'high' or 'low' frequency was frequently wrong, making it virtually impossible that EAP examiners could do an effective running lexical analysis while testing students' oral production.

In the new century, university EAP practitioners face an increasing challenge: marginalisation within their institutions, es-pecially as researchers. In the particular case of the UK, British universities are coming under pressure because of the RAE (Research Assessment Exercise), wherein scholarly output is externally assessed on a five-point scale (the highest rating being five-star). Research ratings have a direct relationship on funding from central government and the competitiveness between institutions has meant the bar has now been raised to securing assessments in the five range: excellent rather than merely very good. This has had the effect of galvanising British institutions to ask academic staff to be more research active, and at higher performance levels so as to ensure that their research is disseminated in, for example, 'high impact' journals. Of course, there is also pressure to attract research funding from external sources.

In such a context, EAP staff members are possibly disadvantaged because their scholarly TESOL (Teaching English to Speakers of Other Languages) activity is in an area which is not usually seen by their institution as being 'mainstream'; few traditionally-minded academic decision-makers in many universities are even aware of the field, or indeed know whether the relevant journals are 'high impact' or not. EAP has a continuing and perhaps uphill struggle for recognition ahead. The institutional impetus for scholarly research is here to stay, and EAP practitioners are not exempt. The days when EAP units were merely seen as providers of student support services (rather than a part of the institution's research expectation) are probably over, though in her article on research methodology in Section 6, Jo McDonough indicates that many EAP practitioners have indeed been active over the years.

Analysing the proceedings of BALEAP (British Association of Lecturers in English for Academic Purposes) conferences (1975–1995), McDonough discerns common methodological threads in EAP research over the years, including the tendency for investigators to use questionnaires and interviews as tools. Text analysis has become increasingly significant, as researchers have studied linguistic/discourse structures and genres, and made use of corpora to support their conclusions. The use of case studies was comparatively rare, while classroom contexts were studied for their 'target situation' potential, rather than for finding out more about overarching educational factors (such as the nature of the process of teaching itself) in general. It is also felt that qualitative/interpretive/ethnographic approaches are underrepresented in EAP research, and the few case studies published remain resolutely local and specific. These gaps imply directions for the future, including studies of (for example), teachers' attitudes to target disciplines and beliefs about language and specialism, and the role and nature of teachers' classroom decisions and determining (via data analysis) what is 'special' about the EAP classroom.

Finally, Keith Morrow addresses the importance of the publication/dissemination of EAP research, providing practical advice about getting published in a refereed academic journal. In addition to providing details of a TESOL website which lists and compares relevant journals worldwide, the author discusses the steps to writing for publication, including being aware of the prospective readership and identifying a substantive topic which evinces an appropriate balance between theory and practice. The article explains the typical phases of the ELT editorial processes, along with an indication of why pieces are frequently not accepted for publication.

This wide-ranging collection of papers demonstrates the growing professional importance and sophistication of EAP in the first decade of the new millennium, while at the same time keeping faith with the primary pedagogical concerns that have engaged practitioners since the advent of EAP as a distinct field of activity and study in the 1960s. Janus-like, the articles also look to the future, not only in terms of the applications of information communication technology in our field, but with regard to an increasing emphasis on analysis of the multiple (and unique) context and learner variables which make an impact on what we do, and where we are, as classroom teachers: to quote an old adage, 'it depends'.

There is something here for everyone.

Leslie E. Sheldon
Director, ELTD (Retired)
University of Strathclyde

Acknowledgements

I would like to thank Jo McDonough and the BALEAP Publications Committee, and express my gratitude to Matthew Oleynik for his thorough copy-editing.

Section 1:
The Profession and its Future

TONY DUDLEY-EVANS
Thoughts on the past and the future of EAP

Good practice in English for Academic Purposes (EAP) perforce involves a practical focus, guided by a genuine desire to find out what happens in the academic courses in UK and elsewhere attended by international students. The primary goal is, I think, to identify the difficulties such students encounter, with a view to designing materials and syllabi which can sensitise them to what departments expect, improve their academic skills and, on a more general level, help them adapt to life in a 'Western' university. There is a requirement to pin down needs by making use of (rather than avoiding) theory and research/analysis. In this article I would like to consider the situation in Britain, which has implications for EAP internationally.

John Swales commented in his final editorial for the journal *English for Specific Purposes* that the ESP movement has not been dominated by ideological debates and divisions arising from single-minded promotion of particular theoretical stances, such as critical linguistics, Second Language Acquisition, or particular approaches to syllabus design (1994). It has retained its openness and eclecticism, and there is little doubt the seminal publications which came out of the British Association of Lecturers in English for Academic Purposes (BALEAP) conferences in the 1970s, '80s, and early '90s (for much of that time named the 'SELMOUS' conferences of course) played a key role in developing this characteristic of EAP work (*ELT Documents*, 101, 109, 112, 129, 131; James, 1984; Adams, Heaton and Howarth, 1989; Blue, 1993).

I fear, however, that in recent years the BALEAP conference papers have had less impact on the EAP/ESP field. I also note that very few papers from EAP researcher/teachers have found their way into the journal *English for Specific Purposes,* or other relevant journals such as *Applied Linguistics* or *TESOL Quarterly.* I am confident original and relevant research is still being carried out, but I fear that the pressures of teaching and concentration on other matters have led to a situation in which the research is not being written up in conference papers, journal articles, and monographs.

I should like to suggest that concentration on both the BALEAP accreditation scheme and on the organisation of pre-sessional courses has played a role in reducing the output of BALEAP institutions. Pre-sessional courses are useful and important, but I have always maintained that though we need to keep a balance between pre-sessional and in-sessional courses, the in-sessional courses that run when students are involved with their subject course provide greater opportunities for the interplay between analysis on the one hand and materials and teaching on the other that was discussed at the beginning of this paper. I fear that BALEAP institutions are in danger of reaching a situation similar to that in institutions teaching Business English. In such situations interesting innovative work is being done, but because of pressure arising from the need to prepare constantly for new courses and new students, little priority is given in teachers' workloads to allocating time for reflection and the writing up of research and materials production projects.

I believe it is essential BALEAP institutions and lecturers maintain their research role and, above all, see themselves as having a vital and original contribution to make to ESP, Applied Linguistics, and even to debate about communication and rhetoric within disciplines. In furtherance of this position I should like to suggest two areas for discussion and research within EAP: rights analysis as part of a critical approach to needs analysis and EAP, and, secondly, specificity in materials and teaching in EAP work.

Rights analysis

The notion of rights analysis has emerged from critical approaches to EAP (Benesch, 1999 and 2001). My interest in a book which includes theory and politics in its title might seem surprising in view of my earlier quotation of Swales' approval of ESP's lack of ideology. What impresses me about the discussion of rights analysis in Benesch

(1999) and the broader discussion of critical approaches to EAP in Benesch (2001) is the way in which the more theoretically oriented ideas of critical linguistics are transformed into practical ideas for the classroom which present a challenge to existing approaches to need analysis and materials development in EAP.

Benesch (1999) describes a situation in an undergraduate psychology class in which students are also attending an adjunct class run by the EAP teacher. The psychology lecturer saw coverage of the syllabus as his priority for the subject course and felt this left no time for questions from students, leading him to put difficult technical terms on the board and giving examples related to the theoretical points. It was clear from feedback in the adjunct class that many of the international students attending the class were experiencing difficulty following the lectures and needed the pauses provided by question time to absorb the material, and the provision of examples to clarify and contextualise the theoretical material. In the adjunct classes the EAP teacher encouraged the students to ask questions and to request examples and emphasised that this was their right. The lecturer accepted this change in focus and at a later stage commented on how much happier and more comfortable the class seemed with greater participation from the international students.

The key finding of this study is that the EAP teacher departed from the usual focus in EAP of discovering the academic requirements of the institution and preparing students to fulfil those requirements. Her role as a 'critical' teacher was to study power relations in the class and seek possibilities for changes in those relations. The argument is that 'traditional' needs analysis reveals institutional requirements whereas rights analysis reveals possibilities for change.

One attractive feature of rights analysis is that it is clearly sensitive to different situations; other classes will have different issues to address. Benesch (2001), for example, shows how the EAP teacher can help students address difficulties with the accumulation of assignments at the end of term.

A rights analysis approach to EAP is clearly sensitive to different situations. The question arises, however, as to whether it would really work effectively outside the USA or even New York. In the situation Benesch describes there is little attempt to allow for the large numbers of international students and the focus of the teaching seems to remain with the native speaker students. It is also a situation in which there have been large budget cuts in programmes for international students, despite the fact that many of these students eventually settle in the USA It is in other words fertile territory for an approach based on rights analysis.

In the UK, on the other hand, it seems unlikely an approach based on rights analysis that encourages students to confront lecturers will work as effectively with students on taught courses as it seems to in New York. I have the impression students on a short master's course (usually one year) are more interested in understanding what is expected of them and then settling down to do exactly that. They are usually convinced protest will harm their prospects, at least in the long term. Furthermore, the dependence of many university master's level courses on the attendance of large numbers of international students has led, at least at University of Birmingham, to some adaptation of the courses and the catering to international students' academic needs.

The situation with research students is, however, very different. My colleague at the University of Birmingham, Richard Cauldwell, sees in his role as academic advisor to international students, a significant number of students with supervision problems. Difficulties in getting to see the supervisor are frequent, as are problems arising from a change in supervisor as a result of retirement. Universities now usually have student charters and codes of practice for supervision, but students do not like invoking the law. They are convinced that if they complain they will lose out academically in the long run. The advisor thus spends more of his or her time helping students develop strategies for dealing with the kind of problem mentioned above than with contacting departments and the actual supervisors. He deals with issues such as how often a student should expect to see the supervisor, how to obtain appointments, and how to cope with suggestions that the student should just 'knock on the supervisor's door at any time' rather than fix regular appointments.

Here an approach based on rights analysis does seem appropriate, especially as the university regulations state problems with supervision will not normally be considered as part of an appeal. The assumption is such problems should be dealt with at an earlier stage. A systematic approach to raising awareness of students' rights of access to supervisors seems to be a valuable extension of the role of the EAP teacher or department.

Specificity in EAP

The second issue I should like to address is of specificity in EAP/ ESP. It is of course a topic which has been debated (often hotly) since the first development of the EAP/ESP movement in the 1960s. Indeed, ideas about how specific EAP work should be have changed quite considerably in EAP's relatively short history. Even today there is a wide range of opinion on this issue, with many advocating a 'common-core' English for General Academic Purposes approach (e.g., Hutchinson and Waters, 1987), while others (e.g., Hyland, in press) argue specific disciplinary features must be addressed in EAP work. I have always advocated working very closely with departments both inside and outside the classroom (Dudley-Evans and St. John, 1998). I am happy to have been involved in both team teaching (Johns and Dudley-Evans, 1981) and team research (Dudley-Evans and Henderson, 1990; Henderson, Dudley-Evans and Backhouse, 1993).

The growing contribution and sophistication of genre analysis (Swales, 1990, 1998; Berkenkotter and Huckin, 1995) provide support for the more specific approaches to ESP. Genre analysis is increasingly showing that different professional communities have their own practices, purposes, and genres. Disciplines are created through the ways members of the discipline construct a view of the world in their writing, and this leads to considerable variation in writing across different disciplines.

In Birmingham we have found it increasingly difficult to run one academic writing course open to students of any academic discipline. To put it very simply and generally, students in the arts and social sciences need the skills of summarising the literature, comparing different sources, and comparing and contrasting ideas, while students of science and engineering need to focus more on discussing results, as well as making and validating knowledge claims. However, even this relatively crude division is unsatisfactory, as different disciplines within the sciences or engineering have different conventions for the reporting of knowledge claims. I have reported elsewhere on the differences between the writing expected of master's students in plant biology and highway engineering (Dudley-Evans and St. John, 1998). Plant biology is an established academic discipline in which student writers need to contextualise their knowledge claims within the ongoing literature and show how their results have made some original contribution to the field. Highway engineering is, on the other hand, a less established academic discipline which has strong links with professional practice, i.e., actual practising road engineers and government departments. The result is that students adopt a more practical approach to writing assignments with the focus on making recommendations for road design and transport planning based on their findings.

I believe EAP ignores these differences at its peril. The greater sophistication of genre analysis today enables us to engage with specific disciplines much more fully and with greater confidence than we could a few years ago. Interestingly, the original work in genre analysis on articles introductions seemed to justify a more general EAP approach (Swales, 1981). If most article introductions in any discipline tended to follow one particular pattern, there seemed little point in engaging with specific issues within different disciplines. An English for General Academic Purposes (EGAP) approach was enough. Though there is still much value in an EGAP approach, I firmly believe it is insufficient and needs to be supplemented by a more specific approach which takes account of disciplinary differences.

Conclusion

In this short paper I have argued that two fruitful areas for EAP research are the use of rights analysis to broaden the range of advice we give to international students, and the degree of specificity of EAP courses. I have suggested a major strength of BALEAP conferences and publications is the balance between theory and practice evident in the majority of papers. Interestingly the two topics discussed reflect these two concerns: one drawing on the pedagogical aspects of EAP (although based in the theory of critical linguistics) and the other based on text analysis. It seems these two complementary aspects have always predominated in discussions of EAP and are likely to do so for many years to come.

References

Adams, P., B. Heaton, and P. Howarth. 1991. 'Socio-cultural issues in English for academic purposes'. *Review of ELT* 1, 2. London: Modern English Teacher in association with the British Council.

Benesch, S. 1999. 'Rights analysis: studying power relations in an academic setting'. *English for Specific Purposes* 18, 313–327.

Benesch, S. 2001. *Critical English for Academic Purposes: Theory, Politics and Practice.* Mahwah, NJ: Lawrence Erlbaum Associates.

Berkenkotter, C. and T. Huckin. 1995. *Genre Knowledge in Disciplinary Communication: Cognition/Culture/Power.* Hillsdale, NJ: Lawrence Erlbaum Associates.

Blue, G. 1993. *Language, Learning and Success: Studying Through English.* London: Modern English Teacher in association with the British Council.

The British Council. 1978. *Pre-sessional Courses for Overseas Students.* London: The British Council, ETIC Publications.

The British Council. 1980. 'Study modes and academic development of overseas students'. *ELT Documents* 109. London: The British Council, ETIC Publications.

The British Council. 1981. 'The ESP teacher: role, development and prospects'. *ELT Documents* 112. London: The British Council, ETIC Publications.

Brookes, A. and P. Grundy. 1988. 'Individualization and autonomy in language learning'. *ELT Documents* 131. London: Modern English Publications in association with The British Council.

Dudley-Evans, A. and W. Henderson. 1990. 'The language of economics: the analysis of economics discourse'. *ELT Documents* 134. London: Modern English Publications in association with the British Council.

Dudley-Evans, A. and M.J. St. John. 1998. *Developments in English for Specific Purposes: a Multi-Disciplinary Approach.* Cambridge: Cambridge University Press.

Henderson, W., A. Dudley-Evans, and R. Backhouse. 1993. *Economics and Language.* London: Routledge.

Hutchinson, T. and A. Waters. 1987. *English for Specific Purposes.* London: Longman.

Hyland, K. 'Specificity re-visited: how far should we go now?'. *English for Specific Purposes* 21/4, 385–395.

James, G. 1984. *The ESP Classroom.* Exeter: Exeter Linguistic Studies.

Johns, T.F. and A. Dudley-Evans. 1981. 'An experiment in team-teaching of overseas postgraduate students of transportation and plant biology'. *Team Teaching in ESP* (*ELT Documents* 106).

Robinson, P. 1988. 'Academic writing: process and product'. *ELT Documents* 129. London: Modern English Publications in association with the British Council.

Swales, J.M. 1981. 'Aspects of article introductions'. *ESP Monograph* 1. Birmingham: Aston University Language Studies Unit.

Swales, J.M. 1990. *Genre Analysis: English in Academic and Research Settings.* Cambridge: Cambridge University Press.

Swales, J.M. 1998. *Other Floors, Other Voices: A Textography of a Small University Building.* Mahwah, NJ: Lawrence Erlbaum Associates.

RON WHITE
The ivory tower in the marketplace

1. The growth of the EAP sector

I would like to begin by considering the development of an English for Academic Purposes (EAP) institution: the Centre for Applied Language Studies (CALS) at the University of Reading.

CALS established in the early 70s at the same time as the first attested uses of the term EAP, and the holding of a joint BAAL-SELMOUS seminar, from which the British Association of Lecturers in English for Academic Purposes (BALEAP) evolved (Jordan, 1997). David Wilkins, then a lecturer in the department of linguistic science, had recognised a need for pre-sessional courses for international students. He obtained agreement from the university to set up a self-funding unit to run a summer pre-sessional course, and he approached regional universities to ask if they would be interested in sending their students to a pre-sessional course at Reading. They were. A market had been established. CALS was born.

From the start CALS displayed features that, with variation, have become common to such institutions:

1. It was self-funding. From the very start, its existence depended on being able to cover its costs and produce a surplus.
2. It was seasonal, so there was seasonal fluctuation in activity and staffing.
3. It encouraged R&D of an applied nature, linked directly to the teaching/service/clientele CALS had been established to provide and serve.
4. It enjoyed an ambiguous relationship to the larger organisation, being not quite 'academic', not quite commercial – in short, not quite 'one of us'.

5.   It established a culture of its own that involved concern for students/customers and a sense of professionalism in its activities.

The first mover advantage enjoyed by Reading and some other universities was soon eroded as others followed their lead, as this is a market sector in which there are low barriers to entry. Within ten years there were pre-sessional programmes right across the university sector; other CALS-like institutions had come into existence, and with them a significant educational and English Language Teaching (ELT) sector had become firmly established.

The considerable size of this sector can be judged from the fact that there are currently 71 institutional members of BALEAP. However, BALEAP is not alone in meeting the needs of international students because – on a broader, national scale – other state-funded institutions have also discovered the potential of the international student market. There are, for instance, 60 British Association of State English Language Teaching (BASELT) institutions offering EAP, and an unknown number of English in Britain accredited schools, including some of the big players to be alluded to later, have started making inroads into the EAP market.

Meanwhile, other changes were taking place in the university sector. In 1992, the number of universities almost doubled, from 45 to 85. This meant that the higher education sector had become more competitive simply because the number of suppliers had doubled. At the same time, the universities themselves were under pressure from that key stakeholder, the government, which, through its various agencies, required the universities to become more efficient in their use of resources (i.e., teach more students with the same or less staff and fewer facilities) while also requiring them to become more effective by measuring up to the requirements of the Research Assessment Exercise and the assessment of teaching quality.

By the end of the twentieth century, the ivory tower had entered the market place, and with it the EAP units had become fully exposed to its benefits – and its dangers.

2. The market

What is the market? Most commonly 'the market' refers to the existing or target group of customers for a particular product or service. A
distinction is sometimes made between the customer (whose role is to
pay for the product or service) and the consumer (whose role is to
receive the product or service). In education, parents or a sponsoring
organisation may occupy the customer role while students assume the
consumer role. In some cases, the customer and the consumer are one
and the same individual. In fact, the market place is one in which dual
roles abound, no more so than in education.

Discussing EAP in such terms as customer group, buyer
behaviour, and function – if not buyer needs – will seem somewhat
curious in the context of an academic conference and of the ivory
tower. Surely the people who enter the EAP unit are students, not
customers? In fact, they are both, since they are not only people
involved in a process of learning, but they are also involved in an
exchange transaction involving the transferring of ownership of a
service to them in return for payment.

What they are purchasing in this exchange is a service product
that has been defined as follows:

> An activity(s) of more or less intangible nature that normally, but not
> necessarily, takes place in inter-action between the customer and service
> employees and/or physical resources or goods and/or systems of the service
> provider, which are provided as solutions to customer problems. (Shostack,
> 1984)

In many services, production and consumption are inseparable,
with the customer being involved in the production of the service, thus
affecting the service process as well as the consumer's perceptions of
service quality. The parallels with what goes on in an EAP course will
be pretty obvious, since both the teacher (the service provider) and the
student (the consumer) are involved in the teaching-learning event
(the process), and it is well known that where there is a mismatch
between the provider's and consumer's solution to the latter's problems, or where there is a breakdown in interaction between the two

parties, the consumer's perception of service quality may be un-
favourable.

The service-product view of educational services does not,
unfortunately, allow for one crucial factor, namely that the service
provider is also a gatekeeper, and that ultimately therefore the
provider will have a degree of power over the consumer that has no
obvious parallels in the service-product encounters in the market place
outside the academy, where the balance of power is typically in the
customer's favour. The ambiguity of the service provider/ educator's
role in the educational context undoubtedly results in a tension in the
provider-consumer relationship which, I suspect, has not been adequately considered in the commodification of education.

2.1 UK market polarisation

Thanks in large part to the increased exposure to English, both in and
out of the classroom, standards of English are rising worldwide.
Likewise, there is greater sophistication among students in what they
expect, and most notably in their use of IT. However, there are fewer
ELT students coming to the UK, and of those who do, more are short-
stay. What seems to be happening in the UK ELT market is a
polarisation into two types of demand and provision:

1. The short-stay UK experience, in which language learning is
    simply one component in a package that includes a social and
    cultural programme. This type of offering is the bread and butter
    of the summer ELT schools operating flexible enrolment pro-
    cedures and two- to four-week courses.
2. The longer term, goal-oriented course, including vocational
    training and work experience, as well as access to higher
    education.

In the state colleges – that is, the BASELT sector – there appears
to have been a growth of foundation course for HE (Higher
Education) courses, either by higher institutions themselves or in
partnership with colleges of further education. Indeed, in state sector
colleges there may be co-operation between the English as a Foreign

KING ALFRED'S COLLEGE
LIBRARY

Language (EFL) unit and other college departments, leading to highly focussed composite courses, combining professional/vocational needs with EFL and new kinds of hybrid qualifications.

3. The chain schools

The polarisation of course provision is matched by a shakedown in the private language schools themselves. On the one hand, there is a growth of the corporate chains that are multiple outlet organisations, distinct from single site operations, though, as George Pickering notes in a recent article, with considerable variation in size, degree of standardisation, product range, ownership structure, culture, position, and growth (Pickering, 2001). On the other hand, there are the small, often owner-managed schools, which vary in size and specialisation.

Pickering suggests what the chains have in their favour is economies of scale and the capacity to purchase and develop specialised expertise in functions like strategic management, marketing, and finance. Large chains also have the resources to invest in major initiatives, particularly in resource-hungry areas involving IT, as well as in internal and external benchmarking activities (Pickering). Small schools find it difficult to compete with such economies of scale, particularly in areas like IT, which requires not only an investment in facilities, but in staff training. Likewise, small players necessarily lack the career development opportunities available in large organisations.

3.1 The seven deadly sins of chains

The chains don't have it all their own way, however, as Pickering reveals in what he calls the Seven Deadly Sins of Chains. I will extrapolate these to the EAP sector.

3.1.1 Local identity

Firstly, there is local identity. In fact, I suspect most EAP units do have a strong sense of their own local identity, to the extent of even a counterculture to the larger organization of which they are a part. Such a local culture can, if very strong, isolate the unit from the other parts of the ivory tower and, instead of seeing themselves as being part of the university, members of the EAP unit may become part of a ghetto – or a dungeon.

3.1.2 Distance from power source

Secondly, and linked to the issue of local identity, is the distance of the periphery from the power source. Because EAP units do not typically offer award-bearing courses, they tend to be out of the academic loop, which usually consists of boards of study, faculty committees, institution-wide committees, and such. This can be seriously disabling because it isolates the unit from the sources and channels of decision-making, just as the branch of a chain school can be left out of the loop because decisions are made at the centre. The solution to this problem is to plug the unit into the command and communication structure of the institution and to work at maintaining its place within this structure.

3.1.3 Departmentalisation

Thirdly, departmentalisation can become disabling if the EAP unit has to work to rather than with other parts of the institution, notably the international office (if there is one), the bursar's department, and even an academic department – typically linguistics but occasionally another discipline. Ideally, the EAP unit should work in close collaboration with the other internal stakeholders and where such a working relationship can be established, both the status and the work of the EAP unit will be enhanced. Unfortunately, this isn't always the case, with the vice-chancellor or some remote university committee making decisions about international student recruitment, or with individual departments taking decisions about student selection, but without taking into account the EAP requirements involved – and resource implications.

On a national scale, the isolation of decisions taken at the centre from the grass roots is illustrated by the so-called Blair initiative that aims to double the numbers of full-fee-paying international students over a five-year period. Any universities seriously taking this policy on board will have to involve the EAP unit because the implications for the numbers of incoming students requiring pre- and in-sessional language support are considerable. Will there be a reduction in entry language level requirements, for instance? If so, how will their EAP language needs be accommodated?

3.1.4 Commodification and depersonalisation

Fourthly, there is the commodification of services and depersonalisation. The initial contacts of an international student with the institution may be with front-line staff whose approach to dealing with customers harks back to an era when students were to be treated as potential delinquents. Fortunately, such approaches to customer service are gradually becoming a thing of the past, but members of the EAP unit may find themselves having to repair such problems. Likewise, the commodification of education leads to expectations on the part of the consumer that the larger institution fails to meet, particularly among students coming from well-resourced institutions.

3.1.5 Weakest link in the chain

Fifthly, the weakest link in the chain. We hope this won't be the EAP unit, particularly if it runs courses accredited by BALEAP. In fact, the BALEAP accreditation scheme preceded the recent higher education concern with quality audits, while the staff development focus of so much BALEAP activity, of which the Professional Interest Meetings are an outstanding example, stands more than favourable comparison with the professional development efforts typical of the rest of the ivory tower.

3.1.6 Titanic syndrome

Sixthly, there is the problem of being insufficiently nimble to respond quickly to market changes. In fact, EAP units are not Titanic-sized vessels, even if the university itself may be, so such units should be small and nimble enough to react quickly to new developments. Unfortunately, the EAP units may lack the information to respond adroitly to market changes. In order to predict market trends, it is useful to have historical data from which to project, as well as information on social, political, and economic trends in the UK and the world at large on which to base decisions. If such information is not obtained and interpreted, the institution, large or small, can be seriously wrong-footed when changes occur. Because EAP units tend to have a captive clientele, in that many of their students are referred to them by other parts of the institution, it is all too easy for them to take such internal clients for granted and to become vulnerable to problems that the university or individual departments have had in maintaining international student recruitment or even in over-recruiting.

3.1.7 Maintaining adaptive capability

Finally, there is maintaining adaptive capability. In fact, UK universities have, over the past 20 years, displayed considerable adaptive capability, but I am concerned that the nurturing of staff talent and morale, which are necessary for maintaining adaptive capability, may be jeopardised by university decision-making processes and by the numerous ways in which members of the ivory tower feel undervalued and unappreciated.

As components within larger organisations, EAP units necessarily have to begin by marketing themselves internally because their first customer is the institution itself. Unless the EAP unit has established and continues to maintain its internal market, it will lack the local advocates who are needed in times of change – especially in a downturn. At the same time, both EAP units and BALEAP also need to address themselves to the external stakeholders who constitute the opinion leaders, policy makers, and implementers in the community at large.

4.   A meeting of markets

The marketplace of ideas is probably more familiar to most BALEAP members than the commercial market of products and services. There is, however, an area where these two markets meet – in the development and publication of EAP materials. Historically, new ideas about methodology and materials have been hatched in EAP centres. It seems to me – given the rather moribund state of mainstream ELT methodology, the blandness of much published material, the evident reluctance of publishers to break out of repeating successful formulae, and the absence of experimentation and innovation in methodology – it is up to the EAP sector to move ELT forward.

One of the functions of the academy is to promote research, and since BALEAP institutions are located in universities, they have a unique setting in which to carry out the kinds of principled exploration and investigation that can stimulate innovation and change. Furthermore, unlike even the large chains, universities tend to have IT expertise and facilities that make possible experimentation and development on a scale purely commercial institutions cannot contemplate. In addition, universities are uniquely placed to obtain research grants for investigations into the application of new technologies. So I would suggest it is in the EAP units that the marketplace of ideas characteristic of the ivory tower and the entrepreneurial drive of the commercial marketplace can be brought together to make a significant contribution to the development of ELT as a whole. At the same time, EAP will have come of age as a significant field in its own right.

References

Jordan, R. 1997. *English for Academic Purposes.* Cambridge: Cambridge University Press.

Pickering, G. 2001. 'Living in chains'. *IATEFL ELT Management* 30, 3–9.

Shostack, G. 1984. 'Designing services that deliver'. *Harvard Business Review* 62, 133–139.

Section 2:
Critical Thinking / Cognitive Skills

JEANETTE LITTLEMORE
Conceptual metaphor as a vehicle for promoting critical thinking amongst international students

It has been suggested international students sometimes need to be trained to question critically the information with which they are presented (Flowerdew and Peacock, 2001). It has been observed that they can be reluctant to question the views of lecturers and authors in their subject fields, and to put forward their own views. This is often attributed to cross-cultural differences in academic traditions (Flower-dew and Miller, 1995) and in argumentation patterns (Connor, 1987). However, in the context of academic listening, it has been shown that an inability to interpret the lecturer's stance in the first place may be largely to blame (King, 1994). Littlemore showed that lecturers often present the evaluative components of their lectures through the use of metaphors, and that international students often misinterpret lecturers' stances because they misinterpret these metaphors (2001). In this article, I describe a study that investigated critical reading ability. International students' critical reading skills were found to be successfully developed through a process in which they were encouraged to identify and criticise the conceptual metaphors that underlie argumentative text.

Before going on to describe the study, it is important to define the terms *metaphor* and *conceptual metaphor*. The simplest way of defining a metaphor is to say that a metaphor occurs when one thing is described in terms of another. For example, in the metaphor 'Her smile was a knife,' the term 'knife' is used to show the author's opinion of a woman's smile. In this example, 'her smile' is the *topic* of the metaphor, 'a knife' is the *vehicle*, and whatever they have in common is the *ground* (Brown, 1958). Here the ground (or means of comparison) might be that both are long and thin, and that both are potentially lethal.

Lakoff and Johnson define conceptual metaphors as 'metaphors that structure how people perceive, how they think and what they do'

(1980). Lakoff and Johnson claim abstract thought is not possible without thinking in terms of something concrete, and that the selection of a particular concrete domain determines how one views the abstract domain. For example, the abstract concept of 'theory' is often thought about in terms of the metaphor 'theories are buildings'. This gives rise to expressions such as 'what are the foundations for your theory?', 'the argument is shaky', 'we need you to construct a strong argument', 'the argument collapsed', 'we need to buttress the theory with solid arguments', and so on. Viewing a theory as a building presumably implies one sees it as something that is strong and solid that needs to be constructed, and that can only be demolished with difficulty.

As we can see from the above examples, metaphors often contain a strong evaluative component. Where conceptual metaphors are concerned, this is particularly important, as the choice of metaphor often reflects a particular writer's view of the world. Through the persuasive use of conceptual metaphors, he/she is able to give the impression that this is the only view available, and it can often be difficult for a reader to question the argument (see, e.g., Mio, 1996). It is therefore likely that if readers can identify the conceptual metaphors underlying persuasive texts, and see the limitations of these metaphors, they may be in a better position to question the opinions of the writers critically. This is likely to be equally true for both native and non-native speakers. However, non-native speakers are particularly likely to benefit from training in critical reading as they may be unfamiliar with the Western academic tradition, which favours 'a type of argumentation which challenges, rather than depends on, textual authority' (Belcher, 1995).

The study

The participants in the study were 30 students studying for an MBA in public service administration in an international development department at a British university. All of them had an International English Language Testing Service (IELTS) score of 5.5 or above. They were divided into one experimental group (N = 15) and one control group (N = 15). Both groups participated in a general 'critical thinking' session. The experimental group was also given a 'metaphoric awareness-raising' session, whereas the control group was given no such session. The aim of the study was to investigate whether or not the metaphoric awareness-raising session had any lasting effect on the critical reading abilities of the students in the experimental group. It was hypothesised that it would. The metaphoric awareness-raising session (which is described below) took place at the beginning of the academic year, whereas the test of its effectiveness took place just after the general critical thinking session five months later. In this way, it was possible to test the long-term effectiveness of the training session.

In the metaphoric awareness-raising session, which lasted approximately 90 minutes, I began by introducing the students to the notion of *conceptual metaphors*. As an example, I introduced the participants to the 'theories are buildings' metaphor mentioned above. I then showed them the expressions in Fig. 1 and asked them to work out the underlying conceptual metaphor.

We then discussed the political implications of conceptualising society as a body, and I got the participants to think of other metaphors that could be used to describe society, and to comment on their political implications. Next, we looked at three conceptual metaphors that are often used to describe the civil service (see Fig. 2).

Society is a...

– Our society is making great strides
– The head of state
– China finally stood up and was counted
– The backbone of society
– The bowels of society
– Spies are the eyes and ears of society
– The voice of America

Figure 1: Exercise given to participants in which they had to guess
the underlying conceptual metaphor

The civil service is a…

A: We need to put together a toolkit.
     The government has pumped in more money.
     He's just another cog.

B: Let's compare input and output.
     We are ahead of our competitors.
     We have a monopoly in this area.

C: We must grow more good leaders.
     It needs to be slimmed down.
     Let's have a look at the core officers.

Figure 2: Conceptual metaphors used to talk about the civil service

---

Lifetime Employment

One of the disadvantages of lifetime employment is you are left with the saplings your father planted. In a time of major change the saplings may be the wrong variety. Turning building societies into banks, or banks into financial hypermarkets may be good corporate strategy but it is hard to staff the new organisations adequately with the people recruited for the old. Inevitably, new talent is brought in, usually near the top and in the middle, making nonsense of the implied promises to earlier staff.

(Saplings = young trees)
(Hypermarkets = very large supermarkets)

What does the author think about lifetime employment?

What metaphor does he/she use?

In what ways does this metaphor work?

In what ways does it not work?

What alternative metaphors could be used to talk about this subject?

Figure 3: One of the texts given to the students

I encouraged the students to guess the three metaphors (a machine, a company, and a living organism) and we discussed the implications of conceptualising the civil service in these ways.

Finally, we examined some conceptual metaphors in context. The students were split into five groups of three, each given a text containing an underlying conceptual metaphor. Their task was to identify the metaphor and perceive its strengths and limitations. They were then asked to think up alternatives to the metaphor.

Each group then presented its ideas to the rest of the class and a general discussion ensued in which further limitations of the metaphors were suggested. The students were able to complete the task effectively for each of the five texts.

Five months later, the students in both the experimental group and the control group were asked to complete a test of critical thinking. They were given two texts, one of which contained an underlying conceptual metaphor. For each text, they were asked to write a critical evaluation of the argument presented, introducing further arguments they judged to be relevant. They were told their evaluations should show they were clear about the structure of the argument (e.g., which claims were reasons, conclusions, and assumptions) and that they recognised the argument's strengths and weaknesses. The text containing an underlying conceptual metaphor is shown below in Fig. 4.

Of the 15 students who had attended the metaphoric awareness-raising session, seven made explicit references to the underlying metaphor and used these references to support their critical evaluations. Interestingly, and in accordance with the hypothesis, none of the students in the control group made any reference to the underlying metaphor. The three examples below serve to illustrate some of the ways in which students in the experimental group used their metaphoric-awareness in order to evaluate the text critically. The language in these examples has not been corrected.

The Ecological Niche

To be viable, an organization must continually receive resources from its environment; the environment is the organization's only possible source of sustenance or energy. A viable organization is an open system which must have a strong position in or a relationship to its environment whereby it receives necessary resources or energy. The position that an organization occupies in its environment is called its ecological niche. To illustrate the ecological niche concept, consider an organization that generally can expect to receive the necessary resources from its environment only if it provides goods or services desired by that environment. The particular place that provides this favourable relationship is the organization's ecological niche.

An ecological niche can be illustrated as a round hole in the environment. If an organization is a 'round peg' that will exactly fit into this round hole, a viable relationship between the organization and its environmental niche will exist. Suppose, however, that the organization is a 'square peg'. In that case it and/or the environment must change if a viable relationship is to be obtained. Such mutual accommodations of environments and organizations are common.

It has frequently been said that an organization must grow or die. However, too much growth may well be dysfunctional for viability if an organization exceeds the size of its niche. The challenge for viability is to adapt successfully to a dynamic environment. 'Grow or die' is simplistic, and may even be dysfunctional. The purpose of an organization in its ecological niche is to provide desirable outputs for the use of the environment. Smaller organizations often perform this function better than large ones. A viable relationship exists if both the organization and its environment are satisfied with the resources provided by the other.

Adapted from Hicks, H. and C. Gullet. 1975. *Organizations: Theory and Behaviour*, Tokyo: McGraw-Hill.

Figure 4: Text containing an underlying conceptual metaphor

In the first example (Fig. 5), the student draws attention to the fact that a metaphor is being used to make a generalisation, and to avoid discussing specific organisational factors, as not all of these would support the argument. She shows an awareness of how metaphors can be used to present half-truths.

It might have been more helpful to *specifically (not metaphorically)* identify those organizational factors or environmental factors which can interact with and support each other.

Figure 5: First example of metaphorically based critical thinking

In the second example (Fig. 6), the student is able to appreciate that the metaphor of an 'ecological niche' can be read on two different levels. It can either be interpreted in a rather abstract way, to include markets, or it can be interpreted in a much more concrete way, to refer to a physical locality. This student is able to see that the strength of the argument depends, to a large extent, on the way in which one interprets the metaphor.

> The use of an ecological system as an *analogy* cleverly illustrates the interdependency of an organization and its environment, but *what the authors fail to do is to fully explain what a niche actually is*. If they are using it to *include markets*, then their argument is a strong one ... however, if 'niche' is meant to be a *physical locality*, then their argument is weak. This is particularly so in the modern day global economy or environment.

Figure 6: Second example of metaphorically based critical thinking

In the third example (Fig. 7), the student is able to identify the *limitations* of the metaphor. She points out that when the organisation is a governmental organisation, the metaphor does not work.

> Some organizations, particularly Governmental ones, have much more power than their citizens. When this is the case, *the metaphor doesn't work as well*. The organization is often *imposed from above*, demands taxes, and the people have no choice.

Figure 7: Third example of metaphorically based critical thinking

We can see from these examples that the metaphoric awareness of each of these students has served to enhance their critical thinking in a different way. The first student was able to point out how the authors' use of metaphor enabled them to generalise, and possibly to oversimplify the issue, the second student was able to read the metaphor in two different ways, and the third student was able perceive the limitations of the metaphor. These findings suggest metaphoric awareness raising can help students improve their critical thinking skills. Future research might usefully examine the role of culture in metaphor interpretation, and compare the metaphor interpretations given by non-native speakers to those of native speakers.

References

Belcher, D. 1995. 'Writing critically across the curriculum'. In D. Belcher and G. Braine (eds.) *Academic Writing in a Second Language: Essays on Research and Pedagogy.* Norwood, NJ: Ablex, 135–154.

Brown, H. 1958. *Words and Things.* Glencoe, Ill.: Free Press.

Connor, U. 1987. 'Argumentative patterns in student writing: cross-cultural differences'. In U. Connor and R. Kaplan (eds.) *Writing Across Languages: Analysis of L2 Text.* Reading, Mass.: Addison Wesley, 52–72.

Flowerdew, J. and L. Miller. 1995. 'On the notion of culture in L2 lectures'. *TESOL Quarterly* 29, 345–373.

Flowerdew, J. and M. Peacock. 2001. 'The EAP curriculum: issues, methods, and challenges'. In J. Flowerdew and M. Peacock (eds.) *Research Perspectives on English for Academic Purposes.* Cambridge: Cambridge University Press, 177–194.

King, P. 1994. 'Visual and verbal messages in the engineering lecture: notetaking by postgraduate L2 students'. In J. Flowerdew (ed.) *Academic Listening. Research Perspectives.* Cambridge: Cambridge University Press, 219–238.

Lakoff, G. and M. Johnson. 1980. *Metaphors We Live By.* Chicago: University of Chicago Press.

Littlemore, J. 2001. 'The use of metaphor by university lecturers and the problems that it causes for overseas students'. *Teaching in Higher Education* 6/3, 335–351.

Mio, J. 1996. 'Metaphor, politics and persuasion'. In J. Mio and A. Katz (eds.) *Metaphor: Implications and Applications.* Mahwah, NJ: Lawrence Erlbaum Associates, 127–146.

ROS RICHARDS
Presenting critical thinking as a study strategy for UK higher education

What is critical thinking and how is it expressed?

There is considerable evidence that some international students and their teachers see thinking critically as a problematic issue in student learning at tertiary level. Fox quotes a Nepalese student:

> What is the process, what is the way we can change so radically here [in a US university] so that we can be accepted, so that we can gain recognition? [...] Foreign students have been getting recognition from the ways they have been thinking and communicating and writing in their previous settings. And all of a sudden they lose all that. You can't imagine what happens to these people! They become very irritated. Very much miserable. (1994)

From the other side, some staff members perceive that international students have difficulty understanding what is expected of them, as the following comments suggest:

> [...] candidates had an overwhelming desire to agree with the propositions put forward in the stimulus statements. Why? They should know by now that the examination setters make up the 'quotes' and they ought to be challenged.
> (*Australian History Examiners' Report*, quoted in Farrell, 1996)

> Students from Malaysia, Singapore, Hong Kong appear to be much more inclined to rote learning. Such an approach does not help problem solving [in dentistry].
> (Samuelowicz, 1987)

Ginsberg (1992) interprets such behaviour in the context of different cultural expectations of education:

In China, knowledge is not open to challenge and extension (by students
arguing with their instructors). [...] The teacher decides which knowledge is to
be taught, and the students accept and learn that knowledge.

These quotations, like many more in the literature, together with
a growing number of research reports (e.g., Atkinson, 1997; Belcher,
1995; Farell, 1996; Watkins and Biggs, 1996), suggest the need to
help international students display the kind of thinking processes often
referred to as critical thinking and expected in Western higher
education practice. Many students will have been involved in analysis
and problem solving in their home countries, of course, but the
suggestion is that the exact nature of such thinking would inevitably
be affected by different cultural perspectives and belief systems.

Until relatively recently, defining critical thinking skills was considered a challenge. In the US, Resnick observed, 'Thinking skills
resist the precise forms of definition we have come to associate with
the setting of specified objectives for schooling' (1987). In 1997,
Atkinson described critical thinking as 'social practice' and
elaborates:

The tacit 'commonsense' nature of social practices is what makes them
functional in a society, allowing members to go on smoothly and efficiently in
the living of everyday life. For precisely this same reason, social practices tend
to resist satisfactory definition and are especially difficult for their users to
describe.

In October, 1999, the UK journal *Teaching in Higher Education*
devoted a special issue to critical thinking, wherein Parker quotes
research which suggests that at sixth form level in Britain, formal,
analytical skills are less tested than they were previously. Perhaps in
response to this, we note that UK secondary education is overcoming
the difficulty of defining critical thinking and is currently developing
and piloting critical thinking material to be taught at sixth form level.
One of the course descriptions, albeit at a particularly advanced level
of study, offers a succinct glimpse of what is considered to form a
grounding in critical thinking:

The AEA (Advanced Extension Award) in critical thinking should provide
opportunities for students to demonstrate breadth of knowledge, depth of
knowledge, an ability to transfer skills and make connections, integrate ideas

and develop concepts, analyse the logical form of arguments, make judgements, assess the credibility of sources, evaluate evidence and examine questions from a broader standpoint than that of a single discipline.
(online: http://www.qca.org.uk/nq/framework/aea_critical_thinking.pdf)

Material is also now available at AS level at a standard appropriate for students halfway through a course of advanced-level study. The aim is to present material 'central to the process of arriving at reason-based judgement', on the basis that 'critical thinking is a fundamental academic competency'. Critical thinking objectives specified include the ability to:

- identify the elements of a reasoned case;
- evaluate reasoning of different kinds;
- recognise and evaluate assumptions;
- clarify and explain ideas; and
- present a reasoned case in a clear, logical, and coherent way.
  (online: http://www.ocr.org.uk/develop/critical/ind-cri.htm)

Similarly, explicit definitions and teaching material are now available on US websites such as http://www.kcmetro.cc.mo.us/longview/ctac/corenotes.htm and, no doubt, in Australia, Canada, and New Zealand.

The objectives described above can be interpreted to characterise the approach required in academic research, specified by Gent et al. (1999) as:

- disposition to enquiry;
- self-awareness and reflection;
- analytical approach;
- depth of study; and
- effective communication of results.

I have taken these characteristics as the basis of a model (Appendix 1), which seeks to show what variables influence the ability of an international student to display Gent et al.'s approach to research (or academic study). The model relates principally to productive skills and specifically to writing within required academic conventions, and accepts that a student's prior educational experience/

cultural identity directly influence his/her ability to deploy the skill characteristics identified by Gent and others, and which relate closely to the objectives specified by secondary school examinations in critical thinking. As Fox argues:

> This thing we call 'critical thinking' or 'analysis' has strong cultural components. It is more than just a set of writing and thinking techniques – it is a voice, a stance, a relationship with texts and family members, friends, teachers, the media, even the history of one's country. (1994)

If we accept the complexity of the model, then it is not always the case that international students necessarily lack the ability to think deeply and critically, but rather that they may be unfamiliar with the cultural norms and expectations for developing and expressing such thought in the particular context of higher education, and/or, more specifically, in the particular context of their subject discipline.

What are the implications of differing cultural perspectives?

In order to understand more about the cultural nature of critical thinking and the challenge it may present to some of our students, it is worth considering three aspects identified by Atkinson (1997) which may have implications for differing cultural perspectives:

1. opposing notions of relations between the individual and the social system
2. contrasting norms of self-expression across cultures
3. divergent perspectives on the use of language as a means of learning

In this paper, I will confine my comments to students who share a Confucian cultural heritage, this being representative of many of the English for Academic Purposes (EAP) students on our courses.

While Western notions of the individual allow, and indeed value, individual self-expression leading inevitably to conflict and competition, Asian values tend towards empathy and conformity (Atkinson, 1997; Scollen and Scollen, 1981; Watkins and Biggs, 1996). Matsumoto sums this up for Japan: 'Acknowledgement and maintenance of the relative position of others, rather than preservation of an individual's proper territory, governs all social interaction' (1988).

Such analyses give us a glimpse of the difficulty, then, of claiming and defending an individual point of view, especially if it opposes what is generally accepted, or if a number of opposing opinions emerge from a group. In short, the originality of expression, which is often sought in the West, may be subconsciously very difficult to express by students from the East. Atkinson cites a quotation from a Chinese textbook:

> We young people have to nourish collective consciousness and to learn to deal correctly with the relationship between personal interests and collective interests. When they are in conflict, we should consciously place collective interests first and personal interests second. (1999)

Expressing one's individuality, then, has not been traditionally encouraged in Asian cultures. Atkinson reports how student writing is seen as a vehicle for passing on knowledge, rather than expressing an individual viewpoint:

> Even at the university level, as Scollen (1991) indicates, Chinese students write in ways that highlight their organic place in their chosen academic communities, and (what may amount to the same thing) their scholarly responsibility to pass on the knowledge they have received. (1997)

This may be compared to Fox's quote earlier, in which he ascribes the process of critical thinking as having a 'voice and a stance'. Shen observes:

> In order to write good English, I knew that I had to be myself, which actually meant not to be my Chinese self. It meant that I had to create an English self and be that self. And to be that English self [...] I had to accept the way a Westerner accepts himself in relation to the universe and society. (1989)

If we consider now divergent perspectives on the use of language as a means of learning, the concept of 'doing to learn' is certainly a cornerstone of Western education practice, with writing seen as a means of intellectual exploration. Academics test their ideas though use of language in oral debate and written argument. Ramanathan cites cross-cultural studies which show written language functions to stimulate and define thought, principally in Western-style education (1999). Again we see that the approach expected of students in UK higher education may diverge significantly from the prior education experience of many of our students.

The following observation, by an Australian tertiary teacher of commerce to international students, is typical:

> [...] it can be difficult to cope, in small [graduate] classes, with overseas students who are reluctant to discuss, criticise reading and express an opinion. (Samuelowicz, 1987)

A collection of reports edited by Watkins and Biggs illustrate and explore the cultural values which underpin the common perception of Asian students as passive, compliant learners (1996). Such misperception ignores the strength of the Asian student, which is to attribute success to effort. Whereas the Western approach more readily attributes success to ability, the Asian student sees directed effort as most successful, related as it is to skill, strategy, and know-how (1996).

In this collection of research reports, Lee Wing On analyses conceptions of learning in the Confucian tradition and concludes that education is considered important for both personal development and social mobility. The notion of egalitarianism strongly influences the perspective that each person is able to achieve educational goals if he or she wants to. Given the attainability of education, the key to success is seen as effort and willpower (1996). This analysis explains the high achievement orientation reported of many Asian students. It also suggests that metacognitive strategy training in particular skills will be well received and can contribute significantly towards success.

How can we support students who need help?

I propose metacognitive strategies for critical thinking be developed for the EAP syllabus, believing an explicit approach is both helpful and appropriate. We need material which unpacks the concept of critical thinking and enables students to see how such thinking is arrived at and how it is structured when expressed or displayed. In the introductory phase of acculturation, when students are particularly vulnerable, such explicitness can help to defuse the political and emotive issues of identity and self-expression bound up in critical thinking and give an understanding of what is required in UK higher education. This needs to be offered with the opportunity to develop and practise critical thinking in a supportive environment, using both previously learned and new study strategies.

In the material we are piloting on the postgraduate Diploma in English Language and International Relations at the Centre for Applied Language studies, we have approached this by asking students to consider four questions:

1. What is the aim of academic study?
2. How is this aim achieved in Western-style education practice?
3. What does this require of students?
4. How is well-reasoned work produced?

Each of these questions was explicitly addressed and we are developing activities to consolidate the learning and understanding involved in each phase. It is not intended this material be used in isolation. The idea is to present and incorporate it into the English language part of the course, where it is woven into the typical activities and assignments, so that as students develop their critical thinking skills through the process of doing (developing cognitive strategies), so the material becomes meaningful and their under-standing of what is required deepens (developing metacognitive strategies). Throughout, they are encouraged to transfer the skills and strategies they are learning to the international relations course material and assignments.

After the four questions were fully considered and discussed, the students were encouraged to work towards effectively communicating evidence of critical thinking in their work. An example of what this involves can be found at Appendix 2. As they became more proficient n this, they reached the stage of being able to choose one of their 3,000-word assignments and use a worksheet to help them follow through the stages of constructing a reasoned justification of their argument. This approach, informed by material at www.kcmetro.cc.mo.us/longview/ctac/corenotes.htm, was positively received by students in their second term of the diploma course, who had to tackle assignment titles such as the following:

> Examine critically the basic philosophy of the main political parties towards foreign and defence policy.

> How valid were the reasons for the British development of nuclear weapons? Assess the motives for and reactions to the 1957 Defence White Paper.

> 'National identity remains basic to personal and social life'. Discuss.

> 'States are as much a source of human insecurity as opposed to a solution to human insecurity'. Discuss.

While these assignment titles clearly call for the discursive writing typical of politics essays, we have collected a number of other assignment titles from around the University of Reading, which could also be tackled using the same approach, at least for discursive subjects in the arts and social sciences.

In this paper I have analysed the concept of critical thinking, and have mentioned some of the cultural issues which may influence the understanding and practice of critical thinking. Likewise, I have noted the potential for adaptability shown by Asian students, through their strongly held belief in the power of effort and will to bring success. These factors underpin our proposed explicit approach to strategy training in the development and expression of critical thinking skills. Such training needs to be offered with the opportunity to practise extensively within the relative safety of the EAP classroom. We need to help students understand what is expected of them, and why – as well as how they can at least develop the foundations of critical reasoning, even within the short time typically allowed on EAP courses.

References

Atkinson, D. 1997. 'A critical approach to critical thinking in TESOL'. *TESOL Quarterly* 31/1, 71–94.

Collins, A., J. Brown, and S. Newman. 1989. 'Cognitive apprenticeship: Teaching the crafts of reading, writing and mathematics'. In L. Resnick (ed.) *Knowing, Learning and Instruction: Essays in Honour of Robert Glasner*. Hillsdale, NJ: Lawrence Erlbaum Associates, 453–494.

Farrell, L. 1996. '"People like us": confronting dilemmas of culture and language'. *English in Australia* 115, 3–11.

Fox, H. 1994. *Listening to the World: Cultural Issues in Academic Writing*. Urbana, Ill.: National Council of Teachers of English.

Gent, I., B. Johnston, and P. Prosser. 1999. 'Thinking on your feet in undergraduate computer science: a constructivist approach to developing and assessing critical thinking'. *Teaching in Higher Education* 4/4, 511–522.

Ginsberg, E. 1992. 'Not just a matter of English'. *HERDSA News* 14/1, 6–8.

Matsumoto, Y. 1988. 'Re-examination of the universality of face: politeness phenomena'. *Japanese Journal of Pragmatics* 12, 403–426.

Miller, L. and M. Connelly. 1997. 'Longview community college critical thinking across the curriculum project'. <www.kcmetro.cc.mo.us/longview/ctac/corenotes.htm>.

OCR ASL Level. 2001. 'Advanced subsidiary GCE in critical thinking'. <http://www.ocr.org.uk/develop/critical/ind-cri.htm>.

Parker, J. 1999. 'Thinking critically about literature in teaching'. *Higher Education* 4/4, 473–483.

QCA Advanced Extension Awards. 2001. Critical thinking test specification. <http://www.qca.org.uk/nq/framework/aea_ critical_ thinking.pdf>.

Ramanathan, V. and D. Atkinson. 1999. 'Individualism, academic writing, and ESL writers'. *Journal of Second Language Writing* 8/1, 45–75.

Resnick, L. 1989. *Knowing, learning and instruction: Essays in honour of Robert Glasner*. NJ: Hillsdale.

Samuelowicz, K. 1987. 'Learning problems of overseas students: two sides of a story'. *Higher Education Research & Development* 6, 121–134.

Scollen, R. and S. Scollen. 1981. *Narrative, Literacy and Face in Interethnic Communication*. Norwood, NJ: Ablex

Shen, F. 1989. 'The classroom and the wider culture: identity as a key to learning English composition'. *College Composition and Communication* 40, 459–466.

Watkins, A. and J. Biggs. 1996. *The Chinese Learner: Cultural, Psychological, and Contextual Influences*. Hong Kong: Comparative Education Research Centre.

Wing On, L. 1996. 'The cultural context for Chinese learners: conceptions of learning in the Confucian tradition'. In A. Watkins and J. Biggs (eds.) *The Chinese Learner: Cultural, Psychological, and Contextual Influences*. Hong Kong: Comparative Education Research Centre, 25–41.

Appendix 1

A model relating critical thinking to academic writing in higher education.

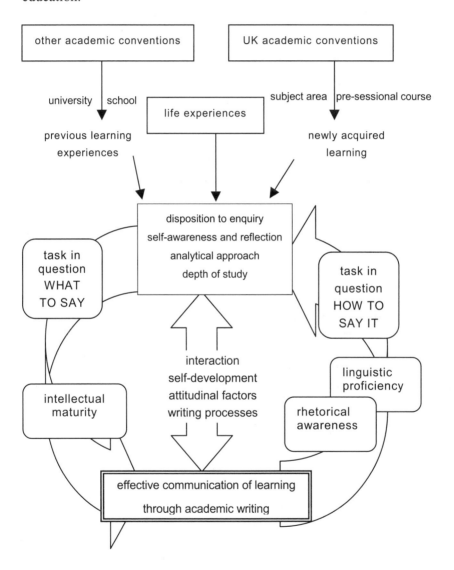

Appendix 2

Example of how students are encouraged towards effectively communicating evidence of critical thinking in their work on the postgraduate diploma in English language and international relations.

Presenting Information:

- Presenting information or argument in a clear, precise, and well-
reasoned way;
- analysing questions and issues clearly and precisely;
- solving fundamental problems set by assignments and/or research questions;
- identifying competing points of view;
- reasoning carefully from a clearly stated factual base or viewpoint;
- demonstrating excellent reasoning and problem-solving abilities,
which take into account the implications and consequences of
proposed solutions.

Contextualising an Argument:

- Understanding and using the key terms and distinctions in a
subject area;
- understanding and using key ideas, assumptions, inferences, and
intellectual processes within a subject area;
- distinguishing between relevant and irrelevant material, and
recognising and using key questions and assumptions;
- using language appropriate to a particular subject area and/or
professional use.

This approach was informed by material at
www.kcmetro.cc.mo.us/longview/ctac/corenotes.htm.

Section 3:
Practical Pedagogy

DAVID CATTERICK
Mapping and managing cultural beliefs about language learning of Chinese EAP learners

1. Introduction

The past two to three years have seen a significant rise in the number of mainland Chinese students joining pre-sessional EAP (English for Academic Purposes) courses in UK institutions. At the Centre for Applied Language Studies, University of Dundee, numbers of Chinese students have increased five-fold over the past two years to the extent that in demographic terms, Chinese students now represent the largest single student group on our courses. The majority of the teaching staff, though familiar with the needs of Asian students from countries like Korea, had very little experience of teaching students from China. Even among the teaching staff who had taught Chinese learners in the Chinese education system, it was felt that these new arrivals could have beliefs about learning different from those of the students who commonly populate university courses in China. There seemed a clear need for a study to determine Chinese students' beliefs about language learning and contrast them with those of the staff.

2. Methodology

It was decided the best way to map learners' beliefs was via a language learning belief inventory. Rather than use Horwitz's general *Beliefs about Language Learning Inventory* (1987), a new inventory (see Appendix 2) was created based on specific comments about the beliefs of Chinese language learners gathered from 11 published sources (see Appendix 1). The comments were collated, then re-worded into specific statements that became the basis of the 30 items in the new inventory. A Likert scale was used to allow each item to be rated and statistically analysed. The new inventory was distributed to 40 Chinese EAP students studying on pre-sessional courses in the University of Dundee and Abertay University. The students who took part were mostly IELTS 4.5 level and above and they were given between 15 and 20 minutes to complete the inventory. They were told that if they encountered any difficult words they could ask the teacher or use dictionaries, and that the teacher was also available to paraphrase the meaning of the items they did not understand. The inventory was also given to 13 staff members who regularly taught the students in the two institutions. The purpose of the inventory was explained to the staff and they were advised that there could be some items that might seem a little strange but that they should complete all the questions.

3.   Results

Once the inventories were completed, the data was processed using SPSS (version 10). A t-test for equality of means was run and the group statistics for each of the variables were as shown below:

Group Statistics				
	Groups	Number	Mean	Standard Deviation
A01	Students (Ss)	40	1.95	0.959
	Teachers (Ts)	13	3.46	1.330
A02	Ss	40	1.83	0.813
	Ts	13	2.38	1.044
A03	Ss	40	1.88	0.911
	Ts	13	2.54	1.561

A04	Ss	40	1.85	0.802
	Ts	13	1.85	1.144
A05	Ss	40	2.48	0.933
	Ts	13	1.77	0.599
A06	Ss	40	1.60	0.810
	Ts	13	2.23	1.013
A07	Ss	40	2.05	0.876
	Ts	13	3.62	0.870
A08	Ss	40	2.55	0.932
	Ts	13	1.70	1.182
A09	Ss	40	2.65	1.027
	Ts	13	4.39	0.506
A10	Ss	40	3.33	0.917
	Ts	13	3.31	0.855
A11	Ss	40	2.90	1.057
	Ts	13	4.31	1.182
A12	Ss	40	2.70	0.992
	Ts	13	3.39	0.870
A13	Ss	40	2.28	0.877
	Ts	13	3.08	0.862
A14	Ss	40	3.03	1.050
	Ts	13	2.62	0.768
A15	Ss	40	2.35	0.580
	Ts	13	3.85	1.345
B01	Ss	40	2.38	0.774
	Ts	13	3.54	1.127

B02	Ss	40	2.33	0.917
	Ts	13	3.15	1.068
B03	Ss	40	2.63	0.868
	Ts	13	3.77	0.599
B04	Ss	40	2.25	0.809
	Ts	13	1.92	0.641
B05	Ss	40	2.58	0.931
	Ts	13	3.23	0.927
B06	Ss	40	2.40	0.982
	Ts	13	3.31	0.630
B07	Ss	40	1.53	0.679
	Ts	13	1.54	0.776
B08	Ss	40	2.88	0.992
	Ts	13	3.62	0.506
B09	Ss	40	2.75	0.981
	Ts	13	3.23	0.725
B10	Ss	40	3.15	0.949
	Ts	13	3.31	0.630
B11	Ss	40	3.15	0.975
	Ts	13	3.77	0.832
B12	Ss	40	3.35	0.802
	Ts	13	4.23	0.832
B13	Ss	40	3.25	1.104
	Ts	13	3.46	0.660
B14	Ss	40	2.33	0.829
	Ts	13	4.00	0.817

B15	Ss	40	2.25	0.870
	Ts	13	3.69	0.947

An independent samples test was also run to test for equality of means and the results analysed for significance ($\alpha<.05$). The items which were considered statistically significant (italicised in the table below) were then categorised and a cultural/notional tag applied to allow for interpretation of the data.

Independent Samples Test (t-test for Equality of Means)				
	t	df	Significance (2-tailed) $\alpha<.05$	Mean Difference
A01	*−3.79*	*16.26*	*0.002*	*−1.51*
A02	−1.77	16.99	0.095	−0.56
A03	−1.45	14.75	0.167	−0.66
A04	0.01	16.02	0.991	0.01
A05	*3.18*	*32.22*	*0.003*	*0.71*
A06	−2.04	17.28	0.057	−0.63
A07	*−5.63*	*20.52*	*0.000*	*−1.57*
A08	*2.39*	*17.13*	*0.029*	*0.86*
A09	*−8.08*	*42.27*	*0.000*	*−1.73*
A10	0.06	21.71	0.951	0.017
A11	*−3.83*	*18.66*	*0.001*	*−1.41*
A12	*−2.38*	*23.03*	*0.026*	*−0.68*
A13	*−2.90*	*20.70*	*0.009*	*−0.80*
A14	1.52	27.80	0.141	0.41
A15	*−3.90*	*13.48*	*0.002*	*−1.49*
B01	*−3.47*	*15.85*	*0.003*	*−1.16*
B02	*−2.52*	*18.11*	*0.022*	*−0.83*
B03	*−5.31*	*29.70*	*0.000*	*−1.14*

B04	1.49	25.52	0.148	0.33
B05	*−2.22*	*20.48*	*0.038*	*−0.66*
B06	*−3.88*	*32.22*	*0.000*	*−0.91*
B07	−.056	18.36	0.956	−0.01
B08	*−3.52*	*40.93*	*0.001*	*−0.74*
B09	−1.89	27.52	0.069	−0.48
B10	−0.69	30.99	0.499	−0.16
B11	*−2.23*	*23.66*	*0.035*	*−0.62*
B12	*−3.34*	*19.71*	*0.003*	*−0.88*
B13	−0.84	34.85	0.409	−0.21
B14	*−6.40*	*20.66*	*0.000*	*−1.68*
B15	*−4.86*	*19.04*	*0.000*	*−1.44*

4. Analysis of the data

The results seemed to indicate that in a number of key cultural/ notional areas the students and staff differed in their stated beliefs. The contrasts cover beliefs as diverse as:

Role of the teacher
- Teacher- /Learner-centredness (A01)
- Professional distance / Personal contact (A13)
- Talent/Lifestyle (A15)
- Native-/Non-native (B15)

Role of the learner
- Learner dependence / Learner independence (A12)
- Intrinsic/Extrinsic motivation (B11)

Teacher/learner interaction
- Encouragement/Face (A05)
- Error correction; Accuracy/Fluency (A07)
- Group work / Teacher-talk (A11)

Language skills
- Declarative/Procedural knowledge (A08, B05)
- Grammar and Vocabulary: Key skills / Adjunct or foundational skills (B02, B03)
- Reading: Vocalisation/Non-vocalisation (B06)
- Writing: Imitation/Creativity (B08)
- Writing: Sentence level / Discourse level (B14)

Classroom content / delivery
- i(nput)+1/i(nput)+2 (A09)
- Deep/Surface learning (B01)
- Systematic/Needs-determined (B12)

Some of the most major contrasts were found in issues with which the staff showed a particularly strong negative reaction to a statement. In item A09 about the teacher choosing content above the level of the learners' proficiency, staff felt very strongly that this was a poor strategy. Group- and pair-work as a waste of class time (item A11) was also roundly condemned. Perhaps the most controversial item as far as the staff was concerned was item A15 about moral lifestyle. While staff members indicated their disagreement with this statement, student responses showed a mean of 2.35 with a high level of agreement indicated by the relatively low degree of standard deviation.

Other results proved surprising for the staff. Item A05 indicated students were less positive about being singled out for praise in the language classroom. While staff members were aware of the concept of face in Asian cultures even those with extensive experience of living and working in China had not expected this result.

5.   Implications

One question raised by the study is why less than two-thirds of the inventory items actually produced statistically significant variation between the groups, despite the fact that the items were derived from published studies. Assuming the original observations of the authors were correct, there are three possible explanations for this:

1. The studies from which the inventory items were taken were dated.
2. The learners who come to study abroad share different beliefs than those who study English at universities in China.
3. Prior to the study there had been some belief shift as a result of exposure to the beliefs of the teacher.

Assuming that despite the relatively small sampling and in the absence of follow-up interviews these findings accurately portray significant belief differences, the implications of the contrasts are quite far-reaching. There are three possible actions that might be used to bridge the gap:

1. Amend learners' beliefs through an explicit programme of learner training.

Though this would make students aware of the differences from an early stage in the course and bring them quickly into line with UK educational values, learner training could be criticised as being hegemonic if not imperialistic.

2. Allow for a gradual belief shift whereby over time the learners' view come into line with the teachers'.

While this non-interventionist stance would seem to offer quite a few benefits, programme directors should still expect criticism of methods by the students in the short term.

3.   Adapt teaching methods to fit learner beliefs.

In an age when methodological eclecticism and client-centred management are very much in vogue, this would seem to be a good choice. Nevertheless, those who take this route may open themselves up to criticism from their staff, which may see the shift in methodological practices as both unprincipled and unprofessional.

6.   Conclusion

It would seem, therefore, that Chinese learners and their Western teachers differ quite significantly in their beliefs about language learning. One issue not considered by the study, however, is whether there is a correlation between beliefs and ultimate success in language learning. Assuming there is a strong correlation, it is clearly not enough to map the contrasts. What is needed is a system of managing these belief differences within pre-sessional EAP programmes. My hope is that this study has gone some way to indicating exactly what cultural beliefs need to be managed.

References

Horwitz, E. 1987. Surveying student beliefs about language learning. In A. Wenden and J. Rubin (eds.) *Learner Strategies in Language Learning*, NJ: Prentice Hall, 119–129.

Wenden, A. and J. Rubin (eds.). 1987. *Learner Strategies in Language Learning*. NJ: Prentice Hall.

Appendix 1

Allwright, R. 1989. 'The social motivation of language classroom behaviour'. In V. Bickley (ed.) *Language Teaching and Learning Styles within and across Cultures*. Hong Kong: Hong Kong Education Department, 266–279.

Bickley, V. 1989. *Language Teaching and Learning Styles within and across Cultures*. Hong Kong: Hong Kong Education Department.

Bond, M. 1996. *Chinese Psychology*. New York: Oxford University Press.

Cortazzi, M. and L. Jin. 1996. 'English teaching and learning in China'. *Language Teaching* 29/2, 61–80.

Dockery, W. 1989. 'Learning English in the United States and English in Hong Kong: a cultural comparison'. In V. Bickley (ed.) *Language Teaching and Learning Styles within and across Cultures*. Hong Kong: Hong Kong Education Department, 55–59.

Dzau, Y. 1990. *English in China*. Hong Kong: API Press Ltd.

Harvey, P. 1990. 'A lesson to be learned: Chinese approach to language learning'. In Y. Dzau (ed.) *English in China*. Hong Kong: API Press Ltd., 168–174.

Lewis, R. 1989. 'Cross-cultural aspects of language curriculum and syllabus development'. In V. Bickley (ed.) *Language Teaching and Learning Styles within and across Cultures*. Hong Kong: Hong Kong Education Department, 458–469.

Li, X. 1990. 'In defence of the communicative approach'. In Y. Dzau (ed.) *English in China*. Hong Kong: API Press Ltd., 116–133.

Maley, A. 1989. 'XANADU – "a miracle of rare device": the teaching of English in China'. In Y. Dzau (ed.) *English in China*. Hong Kong: API Press Ltd., 97–104.

Weckert, C. 1989. 'The cultural and contextual constraints impinging upon overseas students studying at an Australian tertiary institution'. In V. Bickley (ed.) *Language Teaching and Learning Styles within and across Cultures*. Hong Kong: Hong Kong Education Department, 60–69.

Appendix 2

Chinese English Language Learner Belief Inventory (CELLBI)

Instructions
Read the following statements about language teaching and language learning. Show your personal, honest opinion of each statement by circling <u>one</u> of the numbers in the columns to the right. Use the key below to help you.

Key

1 = I strongly agree with this statement.
2 = I agree with this statement.
3 = I only partly agree with this statement.
4 = I disagree with this statement.
5 = I strongly disagree with this statement.

A. Beliefs about Learner and Teacher Roles					
1. The teacher is the most important person in the classroom.	1	2	3	4	5
2. A large part of a teacher's job is to provide learners with knowledge about the English language.	1	2	3	4	5
3. Learners who sit quietly in class will not improve their English as fast as learners who speak a lot.	1	2	3	4	5
4. Learners learn more by finding the answer to a question by themselves than simply being told the correct answer by the teacher.	1	2	3	4	5

5. When a learner gives the correct answer to a difficult question it is good for the teacher to praise the person in front of the other learners.	1	2	3	4	5
6. Learners learn best when they do not speak their mother tongue in class.	1	2	3	4	5
7. A teacher needs to make a point of correcting learners' errors whenever they arise.	1	2	3	4	5
8. A learner can only improve their speaking skills by actively speaking.	1	2	3	4	5
9. A teacher should choose teaching material that is too difficult for the learners and work with them until they understand it.	1	2	3	4	5
10. A teacher should give large amounts of homework to learners.	1	2	3	4	5
11. Spending time speaking English with other learners in class is not good use of class time.	1	2	3	4	5
12. A good teacher is someone who makes a point of being strict with learners who do not seem to be working hard.	1	2	3	4	5
13. A good teacher is someone who spends time with the learners outside of class hours.	1	2	3	4	5
14. A good teacher is someone who makes the learners laugh.	1	2	3	4	5
15. There is a strong connection between a teacher having a moral lifestyle and how well they can teach.	1	2	3	4	5

Please turn over…					

B. Beliefs about Language Learning

	1	2	3	4	5
1. A good language learner is someone who is good at memorising information.	1	2	3	4	5
2. The more words a learner knows, the better their language skills are.	1	2	3	4	5
3. Grammar is the most important part of a language.	1	2	3	4	5
4. Playing language games in class can be useful for learning.	1	2	3	4	5
5. A good language learner is someone who knows a lot about the grammatical structure of a language.	1	2	3	4	5
6. Reading aloud in class is useful for learning.	1	2	3	4	5
7. The most important thing about a language is that a learner is able to use it to communicate.	1	2	3	4	5
8. If a learner copies the style and language of a text, their writing is sure to be good.	1	2	3	4	5
9. The best method of improving pronunciation is for the teacher to say the word and the learners to repeat it aloud together.	1	2	3	4	5
10. Examination marks are the best indicator of a learner's performance.	1	2	3	4	5

11. If the only reason a person is learning a language is to get a good job, that is probably enough for them to be a successful language learner.	1	2	3	4	5
12. It is best to study textbooks in order from beginning to end, not missing out any parts.	1	2	3	4	5
13. When reading, it is good for learners to look up any unknown words in their dictionaries.	1	2	3	4	5
14. If a learner wants to become a better writer all they have to do is make sure they have as few grammatical errors when they write as possible.	1	2	3	4	5
15. A learner can learn more from a teacher who is a native speaker of English than from one who is a non-native speaker.	1	2	3	4	5

ANDY CURTIS
Working with advanced Chinese students:
EAP at the doctoral level

Advanced graduate EAP programmes

One of the earliest reports of advanced English for Academic
Purposes (EAP) in the TESOL (Teaching English to Speakers of
Other Languages) literature appears to be Ostler's questionnaire
survey of the academic needs of what she refers to as 'advanced ESL
[English as a Second Language]' learners at the University of
California (1980). This study was prompted by teachers' concerns
that, in spite of the increasing interest in and use of needs analyses at
that time (see, e.g., Mackay, 1978) 'the teachers had sensed for some
time that many of the real needs of the students were not being met'.
Moreover,

> although the teachers had long recognized differences between graduate and
> undergraduate students, not until the needs survey was completed did ALI [the
> American Language Institute] realize that there were such distinct differences in
> the academic skills required by the two groups.

The important differences between undergraduate and graduate ESL
students at UK institutions have also been reported on, for example,
by Curtis (1996), and by Humphrey and McCarthy (1999).

Casanave and Hubbard note that, in spite of the importance of
writing in the lives of doctoral students in particular, such students
have not been targeted in writing survey research, and they describe
NNSE graduate students as a 'relatively understudied, but growing
(Zikopoulos, 1986/7) group' (1992). Like Ostler (1988) and Paltridge
(1999), Casanave and Hubbard highlight the important differences
between undergraduate and graduate writing requirements, as well as
NSE/NNSE differences, and the issue of discipline-specific versus

general EAP at this advanced level. This paper discusses the concern of materials writers and researchers at the University of Hong Kong to take account adequately, in a pragmatic, needs-relevant way, of subject-discipline and undergraduate/graduate context factors (for example).

Working with students from China

There has been increasing interest in English language teaching and learning in China in recent years (Cortazzi and Jin, 1996) as part of a more general increased interest in language-related studies associated with China (Kirkpatrick, 1995; Yonglin, 1995). Accordingly, the 15th British Association of Lecturers in English for Academic Purposes (BALEAP) biennial conference in 2001 saw for the first time six presentations based on EAP projects with staff and students from/in China (Catterick, Curtis and Cheng, Cutting, Hamp-Lyons, Hassett et al., Kontoulis). Interestingly, then, on the first day of this conference, the opening keynote speaker referred to 'the problem of over-recruiting of students from China by British universities' (White, 2001). Why this was problematic was not explained, but one possible reason for the recent and sharp increase in the number of students from the People's Republic of China (PRC) coming to UK universities may be, at least in part, the result of the relatively smooth change of Hong Kong sovereignty in 1997.

This trend started earlier in the USA than the UK, particularly in certain disciplines such as engineering. For example, Jenkins et al. (1993) calculated that more than half (54 per cent) of the foreign graduate students in engineering departments in North America were from South and East Asia 'with China as the leading country of origin (Zikopoulos, 1991)' (p.51). Jenkins et al. point out that there have been several studies on the writing of undergraduate science and technology students (e.g., Braine, 1989), whereas the writing needs of graduate students in these fields have received relatively little attention. One of the most interesting findings of Jenkins et al.'s questionnaire, sent to engineering faculty at three Midwestern universities in the US, was that 'although the faculty will not accept poor writing, very little effort is made by the faculty to require students to write regularly', which supports Casanave and Hubbard's conclusion discussed above (1992). Other findings from Jenkins et al.'s study relate more specifically to Chinese students, such as the lack of interaction between NSE and Asian students, and one supervisor's telling comment that, in relation to problems with syntax and organization in writing 'I find that all of these aspects are generally worst for Chinese students'.

Snyder concludes with a somewhat prophetic, and in relation to the UK situation, accurate prediction: 'The English language needs of PRC students and academics will continue to present a considerable challenge to the English language teaching profession worldwide for years to come' (1995).

Background to the Hong Kong Polytechnic University (PolyU) programme

The *Effective English for Postgraduate Research Students* (EEPRS) programme grew out of a staff development programme, *Effective English Communication for Teaching and Research* (EECTR), designed to help teaching staff develop abilities to teach and carry out research in English, using a 'reflective genre-based awareness' approach. (See Dudley-Evans, 1995, for a description of this approach used at the University of Birmingham, and see Sengupta et al., 1999, for a detailed description of the EECTR programme.)

As the EECTR program grew and became established, an increasing number of research students asked to make use of EECTR's resources and expertise. However, as EECTR was only for PolyU staff, research students were denied access to EECTR, although an extensive programme of EAP support was available to undergraduates via the English Language Centre. Consequently, the need for a separate support system was recognized and EEPRS was created to identify and meet what was believed to be the considerable need for advanced EAP and English for Specific Purposes (ESP) required by PolyU postgraduate research students working on their M. Phil. and PhD theses and dissertations. Like Richards' (1988) and the UHK programmes, EEPRS was voluntary, cross-disciplinary, and based on a total discourse approach.

During its two initial years, 1998 to 2000, 40 interdisciplinary and discipline-specific workshops were offered, which were attended by a total of approximately 950 workshop participants representing all of the academic departments in PolyU. In addition, around 110 individual, face-to-face mentoring sessions and a number of tailored courses for departments and faculties were designed and presented. Additional support was provided online, and the EEPRS web pages were visited more than 1,000 times between 1998 and 2000.

Workshop series: EEPRS year 1 (98/99)

In the first semester, September 1998 to January 1999, three introductory pilot workshops were designed and presented on an open-to-all (PolyU postgraduates) basis. The workshops were also adapted and presented to research students in building and real estate department and students in building services engineering department. As well a providing initial support to around 150 workshop participants, this enabled us to gather fairly detailed needs analysis data from around 100 PolyU postgraduates on which to base a more extensive series of workshops the following semester. Based on these data, the following nine workshops were offered in the second semester, between February and April 1999:

- Starting Your Postgraduate Research Degree
- Writing Literature Reviews
- Writing Methodologies
- Presenting Your Results and Analysis of Findings
- Writing Discussions and Conclusions

- Writing Abstracts
- Writing Articles for Publication
- Presenting Your Work at Conferences
- Critical Reading for Postgraduate Study

These nine workshops, each presented once, were attended by 258 workshop participants, representing almost all of the academic departments at PolyU. The Likert-responses from the 222 feedback forms completed in the first workshop series show a very positive response from the PolyU postgraduate research students:

Statement 1: I will leave this workshop with some new and useful ideas.
Statement 2: The workshop was well organized.
Statement 3: The activities were relevant and stimulating.

	Statement 1	Statement 2	Statement 3
Strongly Agree	29.3% (65)	40.1% (89)	32.0% (71)
Agree	69.8% (155)	59.0% (131)	66.2% (147)
Disagree	0.9% (2)	0.9% (2)	1.8% (4)
Strongly Disagree	0 (0)	0 (0)	0 (0)

Workshop series: EEPRS year 2 (99/00)

Based all of the feedback provided by the 250-plus workshop participants who attended the EEPRS year one workshop series, we redesigned and presented the following 10 workshops:

- Critical Reading for Postgraduate Study
- Starting Your Postgraduate Research Study
- Critical Reading for Postgraduate Study
- Writing Literature Reviews (Part 1)
- Writing Literature Reviews (Part 2)
- Writing Methodologies (Part 1)
- Writing Methodologies (Part 2)
- Presentation and Discussion of Results/Findings

- Writing Abstracts and Writing Conclusions
- Writing for Publication
- Presenting Your Work at Conferences

Each of the workshops above was presented twice and some three times, making 22 workshop sessions offered in the second year, which were attended by 538 workshop participants, representing all (24) of the academic departments at PolyU.

The Likert-responses from the 485 feedback forms completed in the second workshop series also show a very positive response from the research students:

Statement 1: I will leave this workshop with some new and useful ideas.
Statement 2: The workshop was well organized.
Statement 3: The activities were relevant and stimulating.

	Statement 1	Statement 2	Statement 3
Strongly Agree	33.6% (163)	39.8% (193)	36.7% (178)
Agree	65.4% (317)	58.6% (284)	60.4% (293)
Disagree	0.8% (4)	1.4% (7)	0.8% (4)
Strongly Disagree	0.2% (1)	0.2% (1)	2.0% (10)

Mentoring

In this type of EEPRS support, research students can submit approximately 10 pages (double-spaced) of any section of their theses or dissertations each time for individual, face-to-face feedback. After reviewing his or her text, a member of the EEPRS team then goes through the text with the research student writer.

We stress to the students and their supervisors that the aim of mentoring support is *not* to provide a simple proofing and correction service, but to help the student writer to become more aware of the strengths and weaknesses in their own writing, so they become more able to self-edit. We have also found that many aspects of the research process itself come up in the mentoring sessions, in addition to questions about language and content.

Mentoring is the most labour-intensive and so most costly part of EEPRS, as each mentoring session requiring at least two hours of EEPRS's programme time. However, we have found this does enable us to provide the kind of individualized support and guidance that frequently results in a great deal of teaching and learning occurring much more quickly than can generally happen in a lecture.

As the use of the mentoring service increased considerably, we usually set a 'quota' for any individual student of six mentoring sessions or 60 pages of his or her thesis or dissertation, which helped ensure we did not have 'excessive' input into the final document. Despite the increased use of the service, we were still generally successful in keeping to our target of meeting with the research students within 10 days of their submitting their 10-page extract, which many students told us compared very well with the times required for their supervisors to get feedback to them.

Tailored EEPRS courses for the faculty of engineering

In addition to the 40 workshops and mentoring sessions described above, in 1998–1999, we were approached by the faculty to design and present a 30-hour course (to be presented twice) for their research postgraduates, between February and May 1998. At the faculty's request, the 30 hours was based on larger group 90-minute lectures (up to 30 students per group), supported with 45-minute, smaller group (up to 10 students per group) follow-up sessions. The course was based on the following 10 areas, as requested by the faculty:

- Critical Reading
- Abstracts
- Introductions
- Conclusions
- Literature Reviews

- References and Citations
- Presentation of Findings
- Grammar
- Tables, Figures and Diagrams
- Presenting your research at conferences

The teaching material developed was based on texts supplied by the engineering departments, included examples of 'good' and 'bad' postgraduate writing in engineering, published papers and articles in related professional journals, and written work produced by the course participants before and during the course.

Based on the positive feedback we received from these courses, we were approached again by the faculty of engineering and asked to run a similar course in 1990–2000, but with all work to be done in smaller groups, i.e., no large group lectures and a greater degree of discipline-specific material. As some engineering departments felt it was too soon for their research students to be thinking about writing for their theses and dissertations, we asked each department to provide us with samples of the kind of writing they would like us to focus on, for example, report writing.

The research handbook

Using the additional funds generated from the tailored EEPRS courses, a consultant was bought in to work with the program coordinator to produce a handbook: *Preparing to Write Your MPhil/PhD: A Handbook for Postgraduate Researchers* (Atkinson & Curtis, 2000).

The handbook was a natural extension of EEPRS's activities. It brought together what we had learned about guiding and supporting postgraduate research students, and was a response to requests from research students and supervisory staff asking for a written record of the accumulated experience of the programme. They also expressed the need for some sort of freestanding, self-access guide either for students who did not have the opportunity to attend EEPRS work-shops and mentoring sessions, or for those who did attend and wanted pre- and/or post-workshop texts they could use. In this sense, the handbook attempted to distil the knowledge generated during the first two years of the programme into an accessible, written form.

The handbook was designed to be an *adjunct* to rather than simply a *substitute* for EEPRS face-to-face and online activities. Consequently, it focused on postgraduate research writing *broadly understood*, i.e., not just on the act of getting research results down on paper, but also more broadly as *all the thinking, planning, organising, data collecting, data analysing, etc.*, that leads to the actual putting down of words on paper. The handbook therefore set out to provide an orientation to the general process of planning an M. Phil./PhD research project, as well as more specific guidance on how to write up that research.

Although the future of the EEPRS programme is somewhat uncertain at this time, it is clear that there is a great need for this kind of specialised, advanced EAP support; a need which seems certain to grow in the coming years.

References

Atkinson, D. and A. Curtis. 2000. Preparing to Write Your MPhil/PhD: A Handbook for Postgraduate Researchers. Hong Kong: Department of English, Hong Kong Polytechnic University.

Braine, G. 1989. 'Writing in science and technology: an analysis of assignments from ten undergraduate courses'. *English for Specific Purposes* 8, 3–15.

Casanave, C. and P. Hubbard. 1992. 'The writing assignments and writing problems of doctoral students: faculty perceptions, pedagogical issues, and needed research'. *English for Specific Purposes* 11, 33–49.

Catterick, D. 2001. 'Mapping and managing cultural beliefs about language learning among Chinese EAP learners'. Paper presented at BALEAP 2001 conference. *English for Academic Purposes: Directions for the Future.* Glasgow: University of Strathclyde, 9–11.

Curtis, A. and L. Cheng. 2001. 'Perceptions and purposes: researching and writing in English at the doctoral level'. Paper presented at BALEAP 2001 conference. *English for Academic Purposes: Directions for the Future.* Glasgow: University of Strathclyde, 9–11.

Cortazzi, M. and L. Jin. 1996. 'State of the art article: English teaching and learning in China'. *Language Teaching* 29, 61–80.

Curtis, A. 1996. *Language, Learning and Support: International Graduate Students at a British University.* Unpublished doctoral dissertation: University of York.

Cutting, J. 2001. 'EAP for the Chinese'. Paper presented at BALEAP 2001 conference. *English for Academic Purposes: Directions for the Future.* Glasgow: University of Strathclyde, 9–11.

Dudley-Evans, T. 1995. 'Common-core and specific approaches to the teaching of academic writing'. In D. Belcher and G. Braine (eds.) *Academic Writing in a Second Language.* Norwood, NJ: Ablex.

Effective English for Postgraduate Research Students (EEPRS), Program Report 1998-2000. Hong Kong: Department of English, Hong Kong Polytechnic University.

Hamp-Lyons, L. 2001. 'The challenges of advanced English for academic purposes'. Paper presented at BALEAP 2001 conference. *English for Academic Purposes: Directions for the Future.* Glasgow: University of Strathclyde, 9–11.

Hassett, D., L. Hale, G. Lazar, and V. Odeniyi. 2001. 'Balancing process and product in course design: pre-academic English for China'. Paper presented at BALEAP 2001 conference. *English for Academic Purposes: Directions for the Future.* Glasgow: University of Strathclyde, 9–11.

Humphrey, R. and P. McCarthy. 1999. 'Recognising difference: providing for postgraduate students'. *Studies in Higher Education* 24/3, 371–386.

Jenkins, S., M. Jordan, and P. Weiland. 1993. 'The role of writing in graduate engineering education: a survey of faculty beliefs and practices'. *English for Specific Purposes* 12, 51–67.

Kirkpatrick, A. 1995. 'Chinese rhetoric: methods of argument'. *Multilingua* 14/3, 271–295.

Kontoulis, E. 2001. 'Learning English for Academic Purposes in China'. Paper presented at BALEAP 2001 conference. *English for Academic Purposes: Directions for the Future.* Glasgow: University of Strathclyde, 9–11.

Mackay, R. 1978. 'Identifying the nature of the learner's needs'. In R. Mackay and A. Mountford (eds.) *English for Specific Purposes.* London: Longman, 21–37.

Ostler, S. 1980. 'A survey of academic needs for advanced ESL'. *TESOL Quarterly* 14/4, 489–502.

Paltridge, B. 1997. 'Thesis and dissertation writing: preparing ESL students for research'. *English for Specific Purposes* 16, 61–70.

Sengupta, S., G. Forey, and L. Hamp-Lyons. 1999. 'Supporting effective English communication within the context of teaching and research in a tertiary institute: developing a genre model for consciousness raising'. *English for Specific Purposes* 18, S7–S22.

Snyder, J. 1995. 'The English needs of CUHK's postgraduate students'. *Occasional Papers in English Language Teaching* 5, 37–52.

White, R. 2001. 'EAP: the ivory tower in the marketplace'. Keynote paper presented at BALEAP 2001 conference. *English for Academic Purposes: Directions for the Future.* Glasgow: University of Strathclyde, 9–11.

Yonglin, Y. 1995. 'Trends in the teaching of writing'. *Language Learning Journal* 12, 71–74.

FIONA COTTON
'The lecturer doesn't want my opinion.'
Mismatched expectations: pedagogical approaches

1. Introduction

The stimulus for the preliminary investigation discussed herein involved a Malaysian student completing a master's in information technology who had submitted a major assignment in which all but the first and last paragraphs had been plagiarised from the internet. Each source had been carefully cited, but the student had made no attempt to write in her own words or to critically evaluate the topic under discussion. The subject lecturer gave the student one week to rewrite the assignment. In the individual EAP (English for Academic Purposes) tutorial that followed, I explained to the student I had no idea what she thought about the topic under discussion, to which she replied, 'But the lecturer doesn't want to hear my opinion!'.

The fact that this student had almost completed her course but still hadn't realised she was expected to express her own views supported with appropriate evidence raises several key questions. First, what are the beliefs of postgraduate international students about teaching and learning and especially about the lecturer-student relationship? To what extent do the students' beliefs and expectations differ both from each other and from the teaching staff? How many of the students, for example, hold the same view about expressing their opinions as the student discussed above? In turn, what pedagogical methods are most appropriate to raise student awareness of different expectations about teaching and learning with a particular emphasis on the lecturer/student roles, and to counteract any markedly mismatched expectations?

Although there have been numerous studies which discuss the problem of mismatched expectations in teaching and learning (see, e.g., Harris and Thorpe, 1999; Barker, 1997; Currie and Leggatt, 1965), only a few studies (Jin and Cortazzi, 1993, 1998; Littlewood, 1999) explore the extent to which students' beliefs and expectations differ not only from those of academic staff but also from those of native speakers and other non-native speakers.

Furthermore, there appears to be little research on the effectiveness of different pedagogical approaches to raise awareness of different beliefs about teaching and learning, or to clarify any mismatched expectations students may have about the academic context. In the absence of such studies, an investigation of international students' mismatched expectations of teaching and learning and an exploration of pedagogical methods would seem, therefore, to be appropriate.

This paper is a report on a pilot project in progress which attempts to seek answers to the questions raised. A survey was administered to a group of international postgraduate students and to a number of their lecturers, to try to identify particular beliefs or expectations about aspects of the learning environment and especially about the staff-student relationship, beliefs which directly affect language choices. The belief statements listed in the survey (see Appendix) and responses from lecturers were used in the classroom as a basis for developing teaching activities to heighten awareness and develop reflection on these underlying beliefs and the extent to which these differed from those of the lecturers.

Although the sample is small, the survey instrument is in need of further development, and the results are not therefore representative, it is hoped this report will provide some practical insights into how the key issue of mismatched expectations about teaching and learning might be approached. Before expanding on the methodology used in the project and the results obtained to date, I will review some of the studies which are especially relevant to the project under discussion.

2.   Background to the research project

Difficulties with mismatched expectations of teaching and learning and the lecturer-student relationship in particular are mentioned frequently in the relevant literature. Harris and Thorpe, for example, in an ethnographic study of the experiences of a culturally diverse group of students studying hospitality in UK, found that the lecturer-student relationship was often problematic:

> Our study showed that different cultural expectations among students and staff about such aspects as roles, social distance, duties, rights and obligations seriously affected students' learning. Interaction in student/staff relations impinged on learning in ways that we illustrate below. We suggest that this too is an area that is insufficiently addressed in EAP. (1999)

Turner points out that students seeking explicit instruction about assignment topics and books may simply reflect differing expectations of the Western academic context and the lecturer's role within it (1999).

To explain why students from other cultures have different expectations about the learning environment and the relationships within it, Barker draws heavily on the work of Hofstede and his analysis of cultures on a collectivist individualist continuum, based on power, social distance, and uncertainty avoidance dimensions (1994). Such explanations are also supported by the research of Jin and Cortazzi (1993, 1998) and Cortazzi and Jin (1997) with Chinese and English students. However, Littlewood indicates that beliefs vary widely and warns against stereotyping students according to their cultural background (1999).

There seems, however, to be few studies on the most appropriate methodological approach to clarify mismatched expectations about teaching and learning. Turner emphasises that in order to raise awareness of cultural differences in expectations about teaching and learning it is insufficient simply to point out that such differences exist, and that serious consideration needs to be given to revising the 'framework' of preparatory programs (1999). Wright suggests a number of activities for English as a Foreign Language (EFL) teachers and their students to explore their respective roles and relationships in the language classroom, activities which could be adopted for use in cultural awareness activities (1987). Barker (1997) and Wilson (2001) recommend the study of Hofstede's theories with international students. Similarly, Jin and Cortazzi have developed what they term a 'cultural synergy model' which highlights the contrasting character-istics of individualistic and collectivistic societies. They recommend their model as the basis for discussion without resorting to stereo-types, and avoiding accusations of 'cultural imperialism' (1997).

Implicit in the use of such models is sufficient time for students to make the necessary adjustments, something which is often lacking for postgraduate coursework students, whose workloads leave little time for anything else.

Cargill has developed a questionnaire which both postgraduate research students and their supervisors complete in order to clarify any mismatched expectations about their respective roles (2001). This would seem to put into practice Macrae's assertion that the academic staff, as well as students, should take responsibility for clarifying expectations, making adjustments themselves where necessary (1999).

Wenden reviews the theoretical perspectives on metacognitive knowledge and its relationship with language learning (1998). A person's beliefs about learning can be seen as part of metacognitive knowledge and can affect learning strategies adopted (1998). Wenden confirms that the EFL teacher's often intuitive belief about the importance of active involvement in learning has a solid foundation in learning strategy and learner autonomy research as well as socio-cultural theory. Nevertheless, Wenden highlights the lack of research into the relationship between a students' '*acquired* metacognitive knowledge' and choice of learner strategy (1998; my italics).

Wenden recommends EFL teachers evaluate students' belief sys-tems about learning in addition to their language proficiency needs and then assist students develop awareness of and reflect upon these beliefs. She recommends a four-step approach to include:

- elicitation of learners' metacognitive knowledge and beliefs;
- articulation of what has come to awareness;
- confrontation with alternative views; and

- reflection on the appropriateness of revising and expanding one's knowledge.

Although Wenden's recommendations refer to the relationship between knowledge about learning, and language learning in particular, this approach could well be used to advantage in any course designed to assist students to 'acculturate' to the new academic context.

3. Context of the present project

The present study involved seven lecturers, five native speakers, and 29 coursework postgraduate international students. The two factors which differentiate this sample from other similar groups is that almost all the students work for the defence forces of their respective countries in Southeast Asia and are slightly older than the average graduate student.

4. Objectives of the project

The aims of the study are threefold: to identify the international students' beliefs about teaching and learning in the particular institutional context; to identify the extent to which the beliefs and expectations of the international students and those of their lecturers are mismatched; and finally to use the survey to raise awareness in students of any mismatched expectations between students and lecturers before evaluating its effectiveness as a pedagogical tool.

5. Methodology

A 19-item survey instrument was developed giving statements of belief about teaching and learning. These statements were made over an 18-month period to the EAP lecturer by international students in the postgraduate coursework programs. The belief statements (see Appendix) were generally grouped in relation to three areas: the lecturer-student relationship, academic writing, and seminar skills. Students were asked to respond to each belief statement on a seven-point Likert-type scale from 'strongly agree' on one to 'strongly disagree' on seven, as well as to make comments in support of each response.

The survey was administered at the start of the academic preparation program to 29 international students originating from several Southeast Asian countries, to seven of their lecturers, and to a control group of five native speaker students.

Once the students' beliefs about teaching and learning were elicited through the survey following step one of Wenden's recommendation, the students were then asked to discuss in small groups their responses to each of the belief statements about the lecturer-student relationship in section 1 of the survey. This activity corresponds to the articulation phase of Wenden's model. Students then compared their own beliefs with those of the lecturers, which follows Wenden's recommendation for some kind of confrontation. This was especially the case where students and lecturers' views were markedly mismatched.

At the end of the course, in line with step four of Wenden's model, students were required to reflect upon and evaluate in the course questionnaire, the usefulness of a classroom session dealing explicitly with the mismatched expectations, this time using a five-point scale from 'very useful indeed' to 'not useful'. Students were also invited to make comments.

6. Results and discussion

The survey showed a wide range of views among the students themselves, both native and non-native speakers, about a number of the belief statements, variations which did not appear to be attributable to any of the possible intervening variables such as age, country of origin, or length of time already spent in the host country. Student responses were fairly evenly spread for a number of the statements such as, for example, 11 and 14.

Similarly, the lecturers' views for some items differed somewhat from each other. Statement one, that the lecturer's job is to tell the student everything he/she needs to know to do well in the course, drew varied responses from the lecturers, although four of the respondents qualified their responses depending on what was meant by 'everything'.

Lecturers' and students' beliefs seemed to be mismatched in a number of cases, which would suggest a need for further investigation and explicit discussion with the group under investigation of situations in which the students' and lecturers' beliefs do not concur. Five students, for example, agreed with the statement that the lecturer is the expert and that students should not insult the lecturer in their essays by telling the lecturer things that he or she already knows. Such beliefs may well lead students to adopt an indirect approach in assignment writing in order to avoid 'insulting' the lecturer. Similarly, five students agreed they should wait until asked before speaking in seminar discussion. Lecturers, on the other hand, may misinterpret silence in seminars as a lack of linguistic ability or understanding rather than as a mismatched expectation about turn taking.

Eight out of 29 students agreed that teachers should give students the answers as they are the experts. Such beliefs indicate a need to explore the concept of learner autonomy and the idea of questions with no clear answers.

A number of student comments about the belief statements seemed to accord with the beliefs expected in 'collective' societies, as discussed by Jin and Cortazzi (1993, 1998), and also indicated different perceptions of the lecturer/student role. Comments such as,

'Lecturers should share their knowledge with students so as to assist them do well in the course it is their moral obligation to do so', accord with the paternalistic view of the teacher in collectivistic societies.

The survey also identified individual students whose expectations appeared to differ most markedly from the lecturers on each of the belief statements. Such students may have greater difficulties with acculturation than students whose expectations more accurately match those of the lecturers. Information of this kind enables the EAP lecturer to develop appropriate support strategies for the students concerned.

There was a high degree of involvement by the students during the teaching session discussing the student and lecturer responses to the survey. Similarly, the evaluation questionnaires indicated strong satisfaction with this aspect of the course. Follow-up interviews will clarify further the effectiveness of the pedagogical approach used.

For this particular situational context, no rigid assumptions can be made about the beliefs students hold, since these vary widely. This suggests each new group needs to be surveyed about their beliefs. Where time is of the essence, explicit teaching materials, which require students to respond individually, may be more appropriate than discussion of theoretical models in raising awareness of individual differences in expectations.

7. Conclusion

Despite the limitations of this pilot project, the small size of the sample, and the limitations of the survey instrument, the initial results seem to indicate that mismatched expectations can be identified for particular groups and that greater emphasis on the identification of individual expectations may have important pedagogical implications. The positive response by the international students to explicit discussion of expectations about teaching and learning would seem to justify continued research with larger numbers of students and staff members. Comparative studies of appropriate teaching methodology when dealing with cross-cultural issues would also be valuable.

References

Barker, J. 1997. 'The purpose of study, attitudes to study and staff-student relationships'. In D. McNamara and R. Harris (eds.) *Overseas Students in Higher Education, Issues on Teaching and Learning.* London: Routledge, 108–123.

Bool, H. and P. Luford (eds.). 1999. *Academic Standards and Expectations: The Role of EAP.* Nottingham: Nottingham University Press.

Cargill, M. 2001. Unilearn Discussion, University of South Australia.

Cortazzi, M. and L. Jin. 1997. 'Communication for learning across cultures'. In D. McNamara and R. Harris (eds.) *Overseas Students in Higher Education, Issues on Teaching and Learning,* London: Routledge, 76–90.

Harris, R. and D. Thorp. 1999. 'Language, culture and learning: some missing dimensions to EAP'. In H. Bool and P. Luford (eds.) *Academic Standards and Expectations: The Role of EAP.* Nottingham: Nottingham University Press, 5–18.

Hofstede, D. 1994. *Cultures and Organisations.* London: Harper Collins.

Jin, L. and M. Cortazzi. 1993. 'Cultural orientation and academic language use'. In D. Graddol, L. Thomson, and M. Byram (eds.) *Language and Culture.* Clevedon: BAAL and Multilingual Matters, 84–97.

Jin, L. and M. Cortazzi. 1998. 'The culture the learner brings: a bridge or a barrier?'. In M. Byram and M. Fleming (eds.) *Language Learning in Intercultural Perspective: Approaches through Drama and Ethnography.* Cambridge: Cambridge University Press, 98–118.

Littlewood, W. 1999. 'Defining and developing autonomy in east Asian contexts'. *Applied Linguistics* 20/1, 71–94.

Macrae, M. 1997. 'The induction of international students to academic life in the United Kingdom'. In D. McNamara and R. Harris (eds.) *Overseas Student in Higher Education, Issues on Teaching and Learning*. London: Routledge, 139–142.

McNamara, D. and R. Harris (eds.). 1997. *Overseas Students in Higher Education, Issues on Teaching and Learning*. London: Routledge, 139–142.

Turner, J. 1999. 'Problematising the language problem'. In H. Bool and P. Luford (eds.) *Academic Standards and Expectations: The Role of EAP*. Nottingham: Nottingham University Press, 59–66.

Wenden, A. 1998. 'Metacognitive knowledge and language learning'. *Applied Linguistics* 19/4, 515–537.

Wilson, K. 2001. E-mail correspondence. University of Canberra, Australia.

Wright, T. 1987. *Roles of Teachers and Learners*. Oxford: Oxford University Press.

Appendix

Cultural expectations in teaching and learning

The lecturer-student relationship

1. The lecturer's job is to tell the student everything he/she needs to know to do well in the course.
2. As a student my role is to listen to and remember everything that the lecturer says.
3. As a student I should not question or criticise what the lecturer has to say.
4. The lecturer does not want to hear my opinions.
5. The lecturer is a busy person, I cannot ask him/her questions if I don't understand.
6. The lecturer should be available to help me whenever I need help.

Academic writing

7. You must begin by giving the background and history of the assignment/essay topic.
8. To copy the words of the master is the best way to become a master.
9. I cannot improve on the words of the experts so I must use their words in my assignment.
10. A definition is a definition. I cannot write it any other way.
11. It is important to present all the evidence before I answer the question.
12. The lecturer is the expert. I do not want to insult him in my essay by telling him things he already knows.
13. The lecturer does not want to read my opinions in my essay.

Seminar discussion

14. It is impolite to interrupt when someone is speaking.
15. I cannot disagree with someone who is older or more senior than me.
16. It is impolite to ask questions, even if I don't understand what someone is saying.
17. In group discussions, it is polite to wait until asked, before speaking.
18. The teacher should give us the answers. He/she is the expert.
19. To disagree with someone in public would make them lose face.

MARTHA A. JONES AND ROGER BIRD
Campus language: helping students to understand academic spoken language in the EAP classroom

Debate concerning the exploitation of 'real' data for the development of materials for use in the classroom has been entered into (Swan, 1990; Bird, 2000; Jones, 2000). Should linguists, teachers, and material writers decide to exploit 'real' language, a further discussion involves the approach to analysis of data to be used. Rapid development in computer technology has led to easy access to concordancing programs capable of dealing with relatively large amounts of raw data, revealing patterns of language use. However, there is evidence of polarity of thought concerning the relative merits of corpus linguistics and a discourse analysis approach (Widdowson, 2000; Leech, 2000).

This paper attempts to examine briefly arguments for and against the two approaches, argues that it is possible to integrate both a quantitative and qualitative approach to analysis and attempts to apply this approach to highlight comparative and contrastive features of language used in a variety of academic settings.

Widdowson praises corpus analysis as it 'reveals textual facts, fascinating profiles of produced language, and its concordances are always springing surprises. They do indeed reveal a reality about language usage which was hitherto not evident to its users' (2000). However, he goes on to say that due to the nature of quantitative analysis, the data is 'decontextualised' and therefore not wholly authentic. Leech echoes this point, claiming corpus linguistics 'tends to assemble representative *samples* of the language, or of different genres, without requiring that these be complete texts' (2000; our italics). There appears to be a presumption that corpus linguistics can only operate in isolation employing a quantitative analysis model. This notion is at odds with Biber et al. who maintain corpus-based analyses do indeed depend on both quantitative *and* qualitative analytical techniques and that although there may be a tendency to 'assemble samples', because of the ability of corpora to deal with large chunks of data, many contextual features may be included in analysis (1998).

The self-imposed restriction to a qualitative approach means that what Chomsky (1987, cited in Leech) refers to as E-language (externalised language) is focused on rather that I-language (internalised language). Widdowson comments on this restriction, and believes corpus analysis 'cannot account for the complex interplay of linguistic and contextual factors whereby discourse is enacted'. This may be true if one agrees with Widdowson's claim that 'corpus linguistics provides us with the description of text, not discourse'. However, discoursal language is not proscribed for corpus analysis. Indeed it is the very features of discourse and their inclusion/exclusion in three different genres encountered in the academic community which is the focus of this paper.

Data analysis methodology

The data used in this study consist of:

a)   Lectures in four disciplines: Politics, Civil Engineering, Education, and Biology (compiled by Roger Bird): 43,788 words

b)   Seminars in three disciplines: English Studies, International Law and Business Studies, and one conversation between two students on an open day in the School of Politics (compiled by Martha Jones): 26,357 words

c)   Casual conversation in halls of residence (compiled by Martha Jones): 13,914 words

A model devised by Leech, shown in Fig. 1, below, was used to conduct a quantitative analysis of the data with the view to identifying similarities and differences across the three genres.

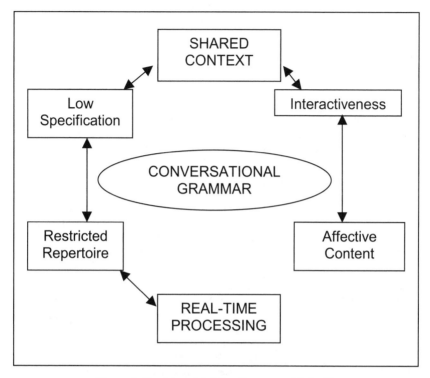

Figure 1: The interrelated functions associated with
conversational grammar (Leech, 2000)

According to this model, different factors are linked to Conversational Grammar: 'Shared Context' and 'Real-time Processing' are the two key situational factors that determine the functional nature of conversation and which also influence language use. 'Low Specification' and 'Restricted Repertoire' are factors more closely related to the linguistic and cognitive nature of conversation. Another characteristic of Conversational Grammar is 'Interactiveness', which means in conversation there is contribution of more than one speaker, discourse evolving through the speakers' joint collaboration, emphasising 'immediacy, responsiveness and reciprocity' (Leech). Lastly, 'Affective Content', closely associated with 'Interactiveness', focuses on the expression of feelings and attitudes.

Leech lists various linguistic features which indicate the presence of some of the above-mentioned factors. The table below includes a summary of these features:

Functional Characteristic of Conversation	*Linguistic Features*
Shared Context	Pronouns, nouns, and ellipses
Avoidance of Elaboration or Specification of Reference	Low mean phrase, high frequency of elliptic genitives, strategic imprecision (i.e., general hedges) 'like' as an adverb, coordination tags (e.g., 'or something'), and low lexical density
Interactiveness	Questions, imperatives, first- and second-person pronouns, one speaker completing a clause begun by another, negatives, 'but', peripheral adverbials, vocatives, discourse markers, attention signals and response forms, greetings, polite formulae, exclamatory components (e.g. 'Oh!'), and expletives
Affective Content	Evaluative and attitudinal adjectives and stance markers (e.g., 'of course', 'probably')
Restricted Repertoire	Heavy reliance on a small list of favourite items (e.g. 'if', 'because'/'cos') and favourite adverbs (e.g. 'there', 'just', 'anyway')
Real-time Processing	Dysfluencies, reductive mechanisms (e.g., ellipses, negatives, verb contractions, 'C-units'[1] (less than six words), the 'add-on' principle using 'and', 'but', and subject noun phrases typically consisting of a single word (a pronoun))

Table 1: Functional Characteristics of Conversation and Linguistic Features (Leech, 2000)

'Wmatrix', a web interface to the 'Matrix corpus tool' (a retrieval and statistical program designed by Rayson, 2001) was used to annotate the data by using a feature of the program called 'Tag Wizard' which assigns part-of-speech and semantic tags. Part-of-speech frequency lists of academic lecture, seminar, and casual con-

---

1   According to Biber et al., a 'C-unit' is used as 'the umbrella term for both clausal and non-clausal units, i.e., for syntactically independent pieces of speech' (1999).

KING ALFRED'S COLLEGE
LIBRARY

versation data as well as concordances using the 'Key item in context' (KIIC) operations were produced to be able to count occurrences of the linguistic features indicating the functional characteristics of conversation, according to Leech's framework.

Two types of quantitative data analysis were used, namely normalised frequencies per 1,000 words, due to the unequal number of words in each sample, and log-likelihood ratio (Dunning, 1993, cited in Rayson and Garside, 2000), using 'Wmatrix'. Log-likelihood ratio is analogous to chi-square, but is more reliable. The findings based on normalised frequencies were presented at the 2001 British Association of Lecturers in English for Academic Purposes (BALEAP) conference and log-likelihood ratio was subsequently used for this paper to identify more accurately the overrepresented features across all genres. For a detailed analysis of log-likelihood calculations, see Rayson and Garside (2000).

Counts of features such as low mean phrase[2] and C-units (Biber) found in the three spoken genres had to be performed manually.

Findings

The results of the normalised frequency quantitative analysis of the functional characteristics and linguistic features present in the three spoken genres used in this study can be viewed by contacting the authors.[3] In this section, we will refer to any notable differences across these genres.

According to Leech, the features which indicate 'Shared Context' are pronouns, as opposed to nouns, and the use of ellipses. Table 2 in Appendix A shows that in casual conversation there is a

---

2   To assess to what extent the mean phrase was low, concordance texts of Noun Phrases were analysed. Pronouns were also included, as suggested by Leech (personal communication).

3   Those interested in examining further detailed documentation relating to this study (including substantial tabular data and the appendices to this article) should contact Martha Jones at Djukweb@aol.com.

higher number of pronouns compared to lectures and seminars, but a certain number of personal pronouns are actually used in lectures, thus reflecting the 'Conversational Style' described by Dudley-Evans and Johns (1981).

However, nouns feature heavily in lectures and academic seminars, and to a lesser degree in casual conversation. The surprisingly high number of nouns found in casual conversation in this sample may be due to the fact that students are discussing not only their personal preoccupations but also their academic subjects and coursework. There is a considerably heavier use of ellipses in casual conversation, compared to the language of seminars or lectures.

In terms of strategic imprecision, as shown in Table 3, there is a certain degree of tentativeness and hypothesis in the seminar setting, while there is less evidence of hedging in both the lecture and casual conversation data. The use of vague language, however, is evident in casual conversation and to a lesser degree in academic seminars. It is worth noting that in lectures this feature is considerably less common, probably because there is a need for more precision in this setting.

To calculate the lexical density[4] the total number of occurrences of nouns, adjectives, adverbs, and main verbs was normalised per 1,000 words. It was expected there would be a high lexical density in both academic samples, compared with that of casual conversation. However, the figures reveal that in fact the highest lexical density was found in casual conversation, suggesting academic discourse contains less fact-based content than might be assumed.

Table 4 shows the use of questions is present as a sign of interactiveness in seminars and to a greater degree in casual conversation. The few questions found in lectures are of a rhetorical type. There are a few imperatives in the seminar and casual conversation data, but these are rare as they would probably be considered impolite. Requests or suggestions are more common. First and second person pronouns are very common in casual conversation, compared with seminars and lectures. The completion of a clause by another speaker is a sign of collaborative effort to construct conversation and is found in both seminars and casual conversation, the latter having a higher

---

4   This method was also suggested by Leech (personal communication). Halliday's formula was not used in this study (1985).

incidence of this phenomenon. The use of peripheral adverbials such as 'actually' is another sign of interactive grammar. 'Actually', more common in the seminar and lecture data than in casual conversation, is mainly used to emphasise what is being said and also to signpost how a particular statement is to be interpreted. 'Well', a discourse marker used in spoken English, is often found in more interactive conversation than in lectures. 'Now' is used as a topic shift marker in lectures, and 'you know' seems to be used in casual conversation more to involve the hearer. As regards response forms, such as 'Yeah' or 'Yes', they are a feature of interactional discourse and are scarce in lectures.

The affective content of conversational grammar (Table 5) is marked by polite formulae, such as 'Thank you', 'Sorry', 'Please', but in our data these were not present. Vocatives with an attitudinal function, such as 'bastard' and 'idiot' were found in casual conversation. 'Oh', 'Ah', 'God', and 'Gosh' are examples of expletives to express emotion, but there were few occurrences of these. Evaluative adjectives, such as 'lovely' and 'good' were more common in casual conversation, compared with more descriptive adjectives used in academic discourse. Stance can be realised by markers, such as 'of course' or 'probably' and by modal verbs. In our data, opinion is marked more in interactive discourse. The most common modal verbs were 'can', denoting possibility in all genres, and ability in seminars and in casual conversation. 'Will' was used mainly to indicate prediction, and 'would' is often used to denote hypothesis in academic discourse but also to hedge statements and to give advice in seminars.

In terms of restricted lexicogrammatical repertoire (Table 6), another feature of interactive grammar, we find that 'if' and 'because' /'cos', are used in explanation. The latter seems to be a favourite item used in casual conversation. Favourite adverbs were 'there' and 'so', and 'just' is particularly common in casual conversation as a hedge.

As regards real-time processing (Table 7), fewer dysfluencies were found in the lecture data compared with the other two samples, indicating a more formal structure, akin to written language. There was a high incidence of negatives in the samples of interactive language, in contrast with the lecture data. Verb contractions are present in the three genres but were particularly common in seminar discussions. As regards C-units, the seminar data seem to have the longest number of words per unit, compared with the lecture and casual conversation samples. According to the 'add-on principle' (Leech), we find 'and' is the most common conjunction in all genres, followed by 'so' and 'but'. Both 'but' and 'because' are more common in casual conversation.

In Appendix B, the sample log-likelihood statistical analysis using 'Wmatrix' (Rayson) to compare two genres at a time shows how this kind of analysis may reveal frequency variation of grammatical or lexical categories between two corpora with greater precision.

Applications

In the light of the above findings, this section proposes possible ways of exploring samples of the three genres in the English for Academic Purposes (EAP) classroom through awareness-raising tasks.

Appendices C and D (http://www.nottingham.ac.uk/~alzmj/ publications/data) include extracts from these genres and a task worksheet, respectively, covering the following features: formality vs. informality, vague language, discourse markers, ellipses, and dysfluencies. It is important to note that for some of the tasks, the students would need to listen to the extracts and read the transcripts at the same time, as the focus is on awareness-raising and not on listening comprehension. It is equally important to be aware these materials are aimed at the more advanced student who already has some experience in using some of the metalanguage included in the worksheet.

Here, we explain the rationale behind the formulation of the questions used in the worksheet. Task 1 focuses the students' attention on preconceived concepts of formality and informality, and in Task 2, the students are asked to listen to three extracts and decide whether their answers given in Task 1 were correct on the basis of features encountered. This type of activity is intended to sensitise students to differences across different genres found in an academic setting. Task 3 addresses the incidence of ellipses and dysfluency, and students are expected to note the lack of such features in the lecture sample. However, Task 4 reveals that other features such as vague language, normally associated with less formal genres, may also occur in a formal setting. This task explains the reasons for the occurrence of such language and invites students to find examples in the extracts. In Task 5, the functions of some discourse markers are described and the students are asked to find instances. It is hoped the students will note that this feature is found in the samples of seminars and lectures but there is only one example in casual conversation. However, this does not mean that discourse markers are not always absent from casual conversation. Such discourse markers are present in seminars and lectures to indicate topic shift and summary and are of importance in enabling students to organise their ideas and subsequently their notes, in the case of lectures, and to understand the content of and participate in academic seminars. Finally, Task 6 invites students to re-consider their initial impressions of the differences across the three genres in terms of formality and informality.

It is possible to develop materials based on a much more in-depth analysis of features of spoken English, e.g., the use of stance markers, fixed expressions, level of directness and indirectness, pronoun/noun ratio, or any other features discussed in the Findings section of this paper. However, it should be borne in mind that fascinating as such analysis may seem to the linguist, such enthusiasm may not be shared by students across different disciplines, and it is essential the linguistic analysis should be instrumental in helping students benefit from the resulting awareness-raising, also mentioned by Jones. Some fruitful exploitation of real language used in an academic setting has taken place with encouraging results, e.g., the Essential Academic Skills in English project (Kelly et al.).

Conclusion

This paper has attempted to demonstrate that the corpus-based and discourse approaches described in the Introduction can *in fact* coexist to yield a comprehensive analysis across different spoken genres from which to develop useful EAP teaching materials. It is hoped materials such as those presented here will help students to notice the features of a variety of spoken academic genres in order to better cope with the communicative demands of academic life. It is yet to be seen whether an awareness-raising approach can be extended to develop materials for students across a range of levels and thus demonstrate further that 'real' data can indeed be of pedagogic value.

References

Biber, D., S. Conrad, and R. Reppen. 1998. *Corpus Linguistics: Investigating Language Structure and Use.* NY: Cambridge University Press.

Biber, D., S. Johansson, G. Leech, S. Conrad, and E. Finegan. 1999. *The Longman Grammar of Spoken and Written Language.* Essex: Pearson Education Ltd.

Bird, R. 2000. 'Academic lectures and the EAP classroom: bridging the gap'. In J. Cutting (ed.) *The Grammar of Spoken English and EAP Teaching.* Sunderland: University of Sunderland Press, 85–98.

Dudley-Evans, A. and T. Johns. 1981. 'Variations in the discourse patterns favoured by different disciplines and their pedagogical implication'. In J. Flowerdew (ed.) *Academic Listening: Research Perspectives.* Cambridge: Cambridge University Press, 146–158.

Dunning, T. 1993. 'Accurate methods for the statistics of surprise and coincidence'. *Computational Linguistics* 19/1, 61–74.

Halliday, M. 1985. *An Introduction to Functional Grammar.* Sevenoaks: Edward Arnold.

Jones, M. 2000. 'Spoken discourse and grammar: the use of real data in the EAP classroom'. In J. Cutting (ed.) *The Grammar of Spoken English and EAP Teaching.* Sunderland: University of Sunderland Press, 55–83.

Kelly, T., H. Nesi, and R. Revell. 2000. *EASE (Essential Academic Skills in English).* CD-ROM. Warwick: Warwick University.

Leech, G. 2000. 'Grammars of spoken English: new outcomes of corpus-oriented research'. *Language Learning* 50/4, 675–724.

Rayson, P. and R. Garside. 2000. 'Comparing corpora using frequency profiling'. In proceedings, workshop on Comparing Corpora held in conjunction with the 38th annual meeting of the Association for Computational Linguistics (ACL 2000). 1–8 October 2000, Hong Kong, 1–6.

Rayson, P. 2001. *Wmatrix: a web-based corpus processing environment.* Computing Department, Lancaster University.

Widdowson, H. 2000. 'On the limitations of linguistics applied'. *Applied Linguistics* 21/1, 3–25.

ZOE KANTARIDOU
Steps to autonomy: curriculum design for a long-term EAP course

Literature review

According to Littlewood's framework the basic components of autonomy in foreign language learning are: *willingness* and *ability* (1996). Our role is to develop a syllabus that provides students (Ss) with the skills and knowledge (i.e., the ability) to make and carry out choices in specific tasks in the language classroom or during the language course which will gradually enhance their motivation and confidence – i.e., willingness to learn. Tasks should be as real-life to the learners as possible and graded such that they provide the skills to change language learners into autonomous language learners. In other words, course designers have to find ways to support the transfer of responsibility for decision-making about learning from the teacher (T) to the learner (Cotterall, 2000). This transfer must be delicately built in and practised within the curriculum, rather than being imposed and demanded from the Ss.

Moreover, Good and Brophy suggest five preconditions for motivation set by the T/facilitator:

• An appropriate level of difficulty
• Learning objectives that are meaningful to the learners
• Variation in teaching
• Feedback about success/progress
• No barriers to learning

This is the framework within which I will try to develop a four-semester English for Academic Purposes course in the University of Macedonia, Thessaloniki, Greece.

Context of study

Greece is an EFL (English as a Foreign Language) country, so English in general and English for Academic Purposes (EAP) in particular serve secondary/supplementary academic purposes. A foreign language (i.e., English or French or German) is a compulsory course in most university departments in Greece, with English being the most popular. The number of Ss in the classroom is about 60–80 and, of course, they are of different levels of competence. Put that together with the kind of negative attitude that Ss have towards state language education as well as the fact that attendance is not compulsory and you end up with empty desks in the classroom. Moreover, Ss are accustomed to a rather passive view of learning, expecting knowledge to be ready-made and filed into their heads by the T.

The study

Within this context, a small-scale research was set out to *ask learners themselves to describe their ideal class*. It was an open-ended question asked to a new cohort of students on their first day to the university. Therefore, Ss did not have time to form any personal opinions on the type of courses available and the course requirements. They were just anxious to start, feeling successful and hopeful for the future. The question was asked to 132 first-year Ss at the University of Macedonia, both boys and girls average age 18.4 yrs, 76 per cent of them at an upper-intermediate level of English.

The answers have been summarised in the tables below:

The teacher should:

Formal training		Personality	
Be able to communicate/ cooperate with Ss	41	Love his/her job	29
Be able to guide Ss	17	Respect Ss	7
Have formal qualifications	7	Be patient and impartial	6
Not do all the talking	2		
Have good pronunciation	2		

The teaching/learning material (the answers can be classified in three groups):

Topics		Skills to be taught		Qualities	
Interesting	6	Vocabulary (mnemonics, specialised, translation)	17	Use of new technologies	31
Academic	3				
Everyday	3	Oral comm.	15	Motivating (humour, variety, novelty)	14
Current issues	3	Business skills	9		
Examined thoroughly	2	Grammar	7	Extra work (HW)	10
		Self-assessment	3	Creative/practical	8
		Listening	2	Organised	7
		Critical thinking	1	Only in English	6
				Advanced level/challenging	6
				Remedial work	4

As far as the S's role in the classroom is concerned:

Ss want:		S characteristics	
To have active participation in class	31	Responsibility	4
		Motivation	2
To have a say on the teaching material	7	Competition	1

The classroom should have:	
A small number of Ss	26
Same level of competence	26
A relaxed atmosphere	17

From these research findings, we can draw a table with the Ss' preferred conditions for learning (Fig. 1) as well as the following conclusions:

- young adult learners (late teens, early twenties) are somehow demanding as customers because they mostly refer to the T and the T/L material;
- they expect their Ts to guide them not only in their learning paths or difficulties but also in new technologies for the novelty and motivation that derives from them; and
- they probably have aims in their minds which are rather general and vague but they definitely don't know how to put them in practice.

Preferred conditions for learning:	
Communication with T	44%
New technologies	23%
Ss' active participation	23%
T motivation	22%
Small number of Ss	19.7%
Same level of competence	19.7%

Figure 1[1]

Thus, our job is to build up a syllabus that is motivating, challenging, creative, practical, and organised in such a way that will give Ss the knowledge and the language experiences they want without imposing our authority and placing the stress of too much work on them. We must love our job and prove it. We must be kept up to date with new developments in our 'trade' so as to be able to make 'principled decisions'. Moreover, we must be able to answer and justify any of our decisions on the basis of shared experience in English Language Teaching, i.e., theories and practice in the literature.

I will describe a syllabus to satisfy most if not all of these requirements. In other words, a *syllabus* that will:

- provide for more than one channel of communication;
- provide for more individual guidance/advice;
- include new technologies and alternative ways of learning;
- require active participation of the learners; and
- provide for group/pair work.

A *task-based syllabus* would fit right in place. According to Willis' Framework for Task-Based Learning (TBL), learners have the opportunity to:

1   The percentages do not add up to 100 because most Ss referred to more than one condition. They are calculated in relation to the total number of Ss to demonstrate the preferred tendencies in the group.

- recall prior knowledge and
- reorganise it with the addition of new elements

in the non-threatening atmosphere of a whole class activity and then

- plan and prepare with their partners or alone for the more exposing aspect of the task, which is the report or the outcome.

This final stage, the language focus, has the advantage of directly pointing to elements of lexis or structure or discourse in the text without openly practising them; thus, it more closely resembles natural learning situations.

In other words, tasks are activities in which the learner uses the target language for a communicative purpose in order to achieve an outcome using any language resources available, rather than practising a specific language form. They require a holistic use of language and mostly higher-order cognitive skills such as critical thinking and self-assessment (Willis, 2000).

The curriculum

According to Dubin and Olstain (1986) the general goals of the curriculum are made evident in their emphasis on one of the dimensions of the syllabus: language content, process/means, product/outcomes (Fig. 2).

In our case the emphasis should be on the process and outcomes of the syllabus, as these are the points most Ss were concerned about (Fig. 1): communication with the T, new technologies, active involvement, small number of students.

Language content	Process/means	Product/outcomes
Familiar topics for confidence *(so that Ss can build the new language structures on familiar knowledge base)* Topical issues for interest Learning strategies both cognitive (mnemonics) and metacognitive (self-assessment, organisation of time and work)	The syllabus is realised in three different means: 1. classroom 2. SAC + Advising 3. Website + Advising In the following combinations: • B or C alone (for more advanced Ss) • A+B • A+C • A+B+C (But not A alone)	List of HW options List of projects Presentations

Figure 2

All the learning material will appear in the Self-Access Centre (SAC) and on a website with suggestions for further study. These suggestions for further study will also be promoted in class from the first semester and Ss will be instructed into the what, where, and how of them according to their needs and preferences. In other words, more autonomous aspects of learning will be integrated into the traditional classroom in order to provide learners with the skills and knowledge – i.e., ability (Littlewood, 1996) – to become, eventually, autonomous language learners.

In addition *advising* also provides a more formal and structured framework for the now-and-then personal comment that the T might give to an individual student. Advising caters for the need of the learners to be treated individually and also paves the way for the less confident Ss to seek personal attention. The basic tools used are:

• a needs analysis questionnaire;
• a screening test;
• a student diary and a T log book;
• a performance portfolio; and
• project work.

The advisor is a specially trained T who must be able to develop and sustain a question and answer (Q&A) process without too much talking on his/her part, resembling in a way the inductive way of reasoning used by Socrates in ancient times. The T keeps a record of every meeting in the logbook stating the kind of problem expressed and the solution offered. The student has a similar record (a student diary), which serves as a kind of learning contract. This learning contract states the tasks and learning objectives the learner has to complete before the next meeting (whenever that will be) and which have been jointly agreed upon based on the need the learner expressed.

With the addition of SAC and the Internet we can release the classroom from some of the tensions that previously appeared there:

- large number of Ss
- different levels of competence
- boredom from the traditional type of exercises

and the demotivation that derived from these

Consequently we can reduce the actual class time since it can be replaced by SAC and the Internet at the Ss' own pace and reserve it for more meaningful tasks and communication in the L2.

By providing three different means of delivery for our course we build in the infrastructure for autonomous learning in the non-threatening environment of a school, so we can hope Ss will learn how to use it also later on in their lives. In this way, we provide for the conditions of lifelong learning.

We will now turn our attention to the outcomes achieved from our language course. The *list of HW options* for each of the units together with the course outline on the outset helps Ss gain a perspective of the learning process in the course and somehow sketch their own path through it. Learners select the pieces of HW that suit them best, either the more familiar or the more challenging depending on their personality and mood.

The idea of incorporating *projects* into the course plan is particularly important. The benefits to be gained are many:

- Ss *develop a feeling of ownership* of the final product which helps them
- *assimilate new information more easily* and
- *identify alternative sources of information.*

Moreover, it helps them

- *associate the course and English in general with useful information* for their studies and the adult society around them, and
- *develop more personal relations with their classmates* through pair and group work and with the T.

The important aspect here is how we develop *autonomy*: the process of gradually releasing T dependence and guidance to leave room for more individual imagination and autonomy (Fig. 3).

1.	2.	3.	4.	5.
Find info with list of questions generated in class	Presentation with resources provided by the T	Presentation with S - produced resources	Class simulations debates	Mini conferences

Figure 3

We can start with guided, simple information-seeking projects such as 'find information about the university library', answering a list of questions generated by the whole class. Then we can proceed into presenting different views on a topic discussed in class with the T providing the sources of information initially, while asking Ss to find them out for themselves later on. Initially, and up to the first year, project work is optional. Ss are left alone to decide whether to participate. This will ideally have a snowballing effect in which more Ss would like to participate in order to share the satisfaction of working with the T and the appreciation of the rest of the group for their work.

Then, in the second year, we can organise whole class simu-
lations or debates in which Ss organise their work in groups or pairs
(info seeking and presentation) with basic guidelines from the T. This
will still give some time to the less confident Ss to gain some
confidence and experience before we pass on to the final stage, which
is complete freedom. There, Ss select themselves the topic, the
sources, and the presentation method to present their work in the form
of *mini conferences*. The mini conferences are supervised by the T but
mainly organised by a group of volunteer Ss who include a proper
conference programme with presentation summaries and time
schedule, audience and chairperson for each session, and time for
questions afterwards.

The way I have proposed it, the curriculum will cover stages one
to three in one year, and then in the second year, stages four and five.
However, that depends on the intensity or the ultimate aim of the
course and the needs of the Ss.

This gradual release of autonomy has the additional advantage of
providing learners and especially less confident learners with the
benefit of 'eavesdropping', i.e., working with or being around classmates who prepare and organise projects and presentations well before
they will have to do them themselves. In fact, they will gather second-
hand experience from their more daring classmates.

Up to now I have considered the need for autonomy as a basic
axiom that can go by without any justification. However, I feel we
need to restate the obvious because it may not be that obvious for
some Ts or in some situations. Adults opt for intensive courses up to
two or three years at the most with an immediate tangible goal of
either a formal certificate or of passing the language requirements for
their degree. Our goal as educators is to provide for further needs as
well, to equip our Ss with skills that will come up handy later on in
their lives when we the Ts will not be around. In other words, to use
approaches and methods to develop the *four I's* as Dudley-Evans and
St. John (1998) put it:

Student
Involvement

can actually reduce rather than raise noise levels as the buzz of active

Interaction

is different to that of noisy boredom.

Individualisation

is not one-to-one attention but allowing each person to be an individual and work and contribute in his or her own manner.

Independence

results from the T allowing Ss to learn in their own ways rather than controlling them through teaching.

References

Brown, D. 1991. 'TESOL at twenty-five: what are the issues?'. *TESOL Quarterly* 25/2, 245–260.

Cotterall, S. 2000. 'Promoting learner autonomy through the curriculum: principles for designing language courses'. *ELT Journal* 54/2, 109–116.

Dubin, F. and E. Olstain. 1986. *Course Design*. Cambridge: Cambridge University Press.

Dudley-Evans, T. and M. St. John. 1998. *Developments in ESP: A Multi-disciplinary Approach*. Cambridge: Cambridge University Press.

Good, T. and J. Brophy. 1987. *Looking in Classrooms*. NY: Harper & Row.

Jordan, R. 1997. *English for Academic Purposes*. Cambridge: Cambridge University Press.

Littlewood, W. 1996. '"Autonomy": an anatomy and a framework'. *System* 24/4, 427–435.

Mozzon-McPherson, M. 1997. 'The language adviser: a new type of teacher'. In D. Little and B. Voss (eds.) *Language Centres: Planning for the New Millennium*. Plymouth: Cercles, 97–109.

Willis, J. 1996. *A Framework for Task-Based Learning*. UK: Addison Welsey Longman Ltd.

Willis, J. 2000. 'A holistic approach to task-based course design'. *The Language Teacher Online* 24/2 <http://www.jalt-publications.org/tlt/files/00/feb/willis.html>.

JOHN STRAKER
What makes a good EAP tutorial?

1. Introduction

The concern of this paper is tutorial teaching within the context of an English for Academic Purposes (EAP) in-sessional programme. For the purposes of the present discussion what is understood by a tutorial is one-to-one teaching in which the principal aim is to assist the student with a written assignment s/he is working on. Both tutors and students appear to value EAP tutorials highly – indeed, in the unit in which I work tutorials are playing an increasingly important part in our in-sessional teaching. Yet the EAP tutorial has quite often been viewed as providing little more than a correction service, a position which has received some support in the literature (James, 1984; Dudley-Evans, 1988; Shaw, 1996). It will be argued in this paper, however, that the association of the EAP tutorial with correction is not inherent to its nature; rather, it is more appropriately seen as a reflection of the low status of EAP within the academy. In particular, the criticism will be that emphasising the limitations of EAP tutorials at the expense of their potential is not helpful. It will be concluded that an appreciation of what this kind of teaching can achieve is the principal ingredient of a good EAP tutorial.

The paper will briefly review the literature giving credence to the view of the EAP tutorial as a correction service, and then report on a survey of the opinions and experiences of EAP tutors and students concerning in-sessional support and tutorial teaching. The survey addresses the issue of the status of EAP in academia and such related concerns as EAP professionalism and identity. Although it relates to a single institution, the suggestion is that the findings may have a wider relevance.

2.   The EAP tutorial as a correction service: a review of the literature

In his case study of a Brazilian doctoral student writing a PhD in the sociology of medicine, James notes how his recommended sub-stitution of 'crumbling' for 'disarticulation' was resisted by the student on the grounds that the latter was a technical term (1984). He adds that the student's view received the support of the thesis supervisor. These observations drew attention to the interrelatedness of subject knowledge and subject discourses, and suggested expertise in the former might sometimes be necessary for assisting the student in the latter.

Research into genre analysis (Dudley-Evans, 1986; Swales, 1990) gave credence to this view, asserting the specificity of subject discourses. Hence, Dudley-Evans argued knowledge of the 'move' structure of a text enabled the EAP tutor to comment usefully on student writing at the level of discourse in subject areas where s/he was otherwise not a specialist (1988), the unstated corollary being that the EAP tutor without such a detailed knowledge of the genre was very much more limited in terms of the help s/he could offer. Shaw affirmed this view, indeed casting serious doubt on the value of tutorial work with advanced students in areas outside the EAP tutor's own sphere of expertise (1996).

Shaw compared his own comments on a student's doctoral thesis in rock mechanics with those of the thesis supervisor, and concluded he was unable to comment in several areas closely bound to the 'essential function' of the dissertation, which in Swalian terms he views as demonstrating fitness to be accepted as a full member of the subject's culture. The areas where Shaw felt unable to comment included content, genre conventions, strength of claim, and technical vocabulary. On the other hand, with some notable exceptions, Shaw did feel able to comment usefully on most sentence-level problems, by which he largely meant grammar and surface features such as punctuation, spelling, and typing errors. In other words, Shaw viewed the 'outsider' (the EAP tutor) as restricted to providing 'some fairly mechanical correction' (1996).

Shaw questioned whether a pedagogic case could be made for such correction, arguing that the way of working in tutorials, commonly a bottom-up process of working through a student's text sentence by sentence, was not conducive to language learning. In any single session a number of points might arise but none with sufficient frequency to enable internalisation procedures to take place. In effect, the type of exposure tutorials offered seemed unlikely to result in development of the student's interlanguage – or so runs the argument. In sum, Shaw is sceptical about the pedagogic value of tutorial teaching in the EAP context, and it seems fair to conclude that he views EAP tutorials as they are commonly construed – as offering little more than a correction service.

3. EAP status, professionalism, and identity: the survey findings

The findings of the survey suggest that in the institution in which they were undertaken the EAP tutors see EAP as a low status activity. In addition, they lack training as tutors and do not agree on fundamentals such as the importance of subject knowledge of the students' disciplines and the value of a background in applied linguistics. Further, there is a belief among tutors that students undervalue their work, although the students' responses offered little evidence for this. Indeed, the students often seemed to have a clearer sense of the purpose of EAP tutorials and of the value of the EAP tutors' expertise than the tutors themselves.

Seven tutors out of a total of nine teaching on the in-sessional programme took part in the survey, and 40 students out of 150, a return of 28 per cent. The tutor questionnaire asked largely open-ended questions, whereas restricted-choice questions predominated in the student questionnaire. The latter was distributed by e-mail. The tutors varied in their contractual arrangements with the institution, three being full-time permanent staff members, and four working on a part-time basis either on fractional appointments or hourly paid contracts. None of the tutors had lecturer status in the institution. The majority of students were undertaking taught masters' programmes and commonly sought tutorials to discuss essay drafts. The survey findings testify to the importance tutors and students attach to tutorials. The tutors' replies included such language as 'important', 'very important', 'highly important', 'crucial', and 'I get the feeling students really benefit from them', whereas 88 per cent of students considered tutorials 'very important / important'.

The tutors were asked whether there was any truth in the claim that EAP tutorials were just a correction service. All denied this, although three suggested this was how they felt they were often viewed by students. One countered the claim emotively, exclaiming, 'From my view – no! no! no! Sad reality is that many students perceive us to be just that'. Others also emphasised the negative associations of correction. One spoke of being viewed as a 'correction machine', another that a correction service could be dangerous. Only one seemed at ease with the idea of correction, replying 'It's *part* of the service only'.

Table 1 shows how the students responded to the question concerning the purpose of tutorials ranked on a five-point scale. The results do not support the view that the students viewed tutorials as a correction service. For instance, 31 per cent considered proofreading 'very important / important'. This contrasted with the 83 per cent who considered commenting on the overall structure of the essay 'very important / important', the item scoring highest.

Asked whether the status of EAP tutors with respect to mainstream academic staff affected their work, four tutors replied that it did. One said it did not and one claimed to have no 'hard evidence' either way. Another felt it affected 'our self-perception' but not 'our work'. One tutor spoke of the poor career prospects within EAP which limit 'one's commitment to / investment in the field'. Again emotive language is used; for instance a tutor replied, 'Absolutely. We are often seen "merely" as TEFL teachers. We are often younger than mainstream academic staff and are not doctors – alters students' perception of us'.

Various questions explored the importance to tutorial work of subject expertise in one or other of the disciplines taught in the

	Very important	Important	Quite important	Not very important	Not important
Check bibliographies and referencing	20	2.5	40	27.5	10
Check 'borrowings' blend into the text	13.2	26.3	26.3	34.2	–
Check content is appropriate	21.5	21.5	35	11	11
Check grammar and vocabulary	43.5	23	20.5	13	–
Check work is OK to hand in	33	23	20.5	15.5	8
Comment on balance between descriptive/ analytical writing	35	32.5	20	10	2.5
Comment on logical coherence	50	17.5	22.5	7.5	2.5
Comment on overall essay structure	50	32.5	15	2.5	–
Comment on paragraph structure	39	34	19.5	7.5	–
Discuss subject tutors' feedback comments	29	26.5	26.5	13	5
Help in initial essay planning	23	20.5	28	20.5	8
Proofread work	15.5	15.5	43.5	20.5	5
Suggest alternative ways of saying things	36	38.5	15.5	10	–
Resolve doubts concerning the university's expectations	25	22.5	27.5	17.5	7.5
Say if arguments are adequately supported	22.5	32.5	42.5	–	2.5

Table 1: Students' views concerning the purposes of tutorial feedback on essays (expressed in percentages)

sciences, 'insider' knowledge of the institution (gained, for example, by virtue of being current or ex-students themselves), and the value of a background in applied linguistics. To some extent the replies reflected the tutors' own backgrounds. For example, while all tutors were experienced English language teachers, two were principally interested in fields other than applied linguistics, while a third had pursued postgraduate studies in another area in addition to applied linguistics.

With respect to subject expertise, three tutors asserted its importance ('invaluable', 'adds credibility', 'enables me to empathise with students'), a further three viewed it as helpful though not essential, while only one did not consider it important. In answer to a related question concerning what they viewed as the main constraints on them as tutors, three mentioned specifically the lack of subject knowledge while a further two spoke of the need to work more closely with subject departments. Those who had 'insider knowledge' not surprisingly tended to view it favourably.

In terms of the value of a background in applied linguistics the tutors' response largely mirrored their response to the question concerning subject expertise. There were those who viewed it as essential and those who did not consider it necessary, with two tutors falling into each camp. Given the background of the tutors this was perhaps not surprising. Of more interest were the replies of the remaining three tutors who were circumspect as to the value of applied linguistics. One considered it 'useful' but 'hands-on experience [...] paramount', another as 'increasing adaptability', the third 'helpful'. These replies are revealing in that there is no strong sense that the tutors as a group viewed applied linguistics as the core discipline informing their work; indeed, the contrary impression is given.

The students' responses to the question concerning the purpose of tutorials (see Table 1) suggest they viewed the EAP tutor as primarily a language expert and in particular someone who could advise on coherence. The highest scoring items in the categories 'very important / important' ('comment on overall essay structure', 'suggest alternative ways of saying things', and 'comment on paragraph structure') all emphasise meaning rather than form. The students were less concerned with grammar/vocabulary per se and do not usually expect the EAP tutor to be able to advise on content.

The students' responses to other questions further evidenced how they viewed the question of expertise within their academic fields. Asked whether EAP tutors could comment usefully on essays in different subject areas, 90 per cent believed they could or could to some extent. To a question concerning the ability of their EAP tutor to understand the subject matter of their essays, 100 per cent believed s/he always or nearly always could. In one of the few open-ended questions the students were asked to suggest ways in which tutorials could be improved. Sixteen per cent suggested the provision of tutors who were experts in their particular fields; this contrasted to the 23 per cent who recommended increasing the number of tutorials – the highest scoring item. These figures do not suggest that the students expect the EAP tutor to be an expert in their own academic disciplines or consider it a great handicap if they are not.

Overall the survey findings suggest the students do not share the tutors' anxieties. The students who responded to the survey do not in general see EAP tutorials as a correction service and are very much less concerned about expertise in their disciplinary areas than the tutors. The tutors' replies, however, do suggest that the majority view EAP as a low status activity, have a variable professional commitment to EAP, and have very different views on fundamental issues.

4. Conclusion

Holliday (1994) attests to the low status of English as a Foreign Language (EFL) within university education, explaining this in terms of Bernstein's (1971) distinction between integrationist and collectionist educational cultures. In the collectionist educational culture subject boundaries are sharply defined and subject expertise highly valued, whereas in the integrationalist culture subject boundaries are less clear cut and expertise often seen in terms of teaching methodology. Holliday argues universities are essentially collectionist whereas EFL is integrationist; he sees this as accounting for the low status of EFL in academia. I suggest that the low status associations of EFL have transferred to EAP.

The English language teaching 'tree' (Hutchinson and Waters, 1987) sees EFL as dividing into General English (GE) and English for Specific Purposes (ESP), with EAP a branch of the latter. The remit of ESP, that of providing students with the language they need for their specific circumstances, is seen to transfer to EAP, hence the concern among such writers as James (1984), Dudley-Evans (1988), and Shaw (1996) to furnish answers, as well as their frustration in not always being able to do so. I would argue, however, that the restrictions imposed by this perspective have obscured the potential of EAP tutorials. Indeed, events seen by both James and Shaw as manifesting the shortcomings of tutorials could equally be construed as exemplifying the benefits of tutorial interaction. For instance, James' negotiation with his student over the term 'disarticulation' would have provided valuable insights into the subject specificity of the student's subject discourse, adding to the student's understanding of the language of his subject matter. In sum, EAP's association with EFL/ESP does not seem to have always served it well and it may be time to seek recourse in an alternative paradigm.

EAP tutorials are as much about raising issues as providing answers. The EAP tutor's expertise amounts to helping students understand how language constructs meaning, and by working with students *on* their texts students learn how to work *with* texts. They become more aware of their weaknesses and what the expectations on them are, knowledge that should help them become more independent as writers. It is this dialogic potential of tutorials that makes them so valuable and good tutorial teaching needs to be based on a recognition of this. The logic that the nature of EAP restricts EAP tutorials to low-level tasks is based on the assumption that academic discourse is like Airspeak: that EAP is little different from ESP. I believe this is a limiting view. I prefer to view the negative associations attached to EAP tutorials as a reflection of EAP's status rather than inherent to their nature. By affirming the value of EAP tutorials those negative associations can be shed, and at the same time a small contribution be made to raising the status of the profession.

References

Bernstein, B. 1971. 'On the classification and framing of educational knowledge'. In M. Young (ed.) *Knowledge and Control*, London: Collier, 46–69.

Brookes, A. and P. Grundy (eds.). 1988. *Individualization and Autonomy in Language Learning*. London: Modern English Publications.

Coulthard, M. (ed.). 1986. *Talking About Text. ELR Monograph* 13, University of Birmingham.

Dudley-Evans, T. 1986. 'Genre analysis: an investigation of the introduction and discussion sections of MSc dissertations'. In M. Coulthard (ed.) *Talking About Text. ELR Monograph* 13, University of Birmingham, 128–145.

Dudley-Evans, T. 1988. 'One-to-one supervision of students writing in MSc or PhD theses'. In A. Brookes and P. Grundy (eds.) *Individualization and Autonomy in Language Learning*. London: Modern English Publications, 136–141.

Hewings, M. and T. Dudley-Evans. 1996. *Evaluation and Course Design in EAP*. Hemel Hempstead: Phoenix ELT.

Holliday, A. 1994. *Appropriate Methodology and Social Context.* Cambridge: Cambridge University Press

Hutchinson, T. and A. Waters. 1987. *English for Specific Purposes.* Cambridge: Cambridge University Press.

James, K. 1984. 'The writing of theses by speakers of English as a foreign language: the results of a case study'. In R. Williams, J. Swales, and J. Kirkham (eds.) *Common ground: Shared interests in ESP and communications studies. ELT Documents* 117, Oxford: Pergamon Press and the British Council, 99–113.

Shaw, P. 1996. 'One-to-one work on dissertations: effectiveness of correction and efficiency of pedagogy'. In M. Hewings and T. Dudley-Evans (eds.) *Evaluation and Course Design in EAP.* Hemel Hempstead: Phoenix ELT, 86–95.

Swales, J. 1990. *Genre Analysis: English in academic and research settings.* Cambridge: Cambridge University Press.

Williams, R., J. Swales, and J. Kirkman. (eds.). 1984. *Common ground: Shared interests in ESP and communications studies. ELT Documents* 117, Oxford: Pergamon Press and the British Council.

Young, M. (ed.). 1971. *Knowledge and Control.* London: Collier.

Section 4:
Writing for Academic Purposes

KENNETH ANDERSON, CATHY BENSON,
AND TONY LYNCH
Feedback on writing: attitudes and uptake

1. Introduction

1.1 General background

This exploratory study focuses on students' attitudes to feedback on writing, and on when, how, and to what extent they act on it. For reasons of space, we will focus on the details and findings of our study so far, and omit the literature review presented in the original version of this paper at the Glasgow conference.[1]

1.2. The 'Academic English' course

Our study was carried out at the Institute for Applied Language Studies (IALS) in the April–June term, 2000. The students we selected as subjects were attending 'Academic English', a five-hours-per-week option within a full-time English as a Foreign Language programme. The term's syllabus was based on individual and group projects. Project work, in which the students identify and research a topic, draft, receive tutor feedback, and revise, has many benefits within a pre-sessional English for Academic Purposes (EAP) course; in particular:

- simulating the 'target tasks' that most EAP students will undertake on their degree programmes;
- providing natural opportunities within a communicative task cycle for *Focus on Form* (Long, 1991).

---

1   The authors will be happy to provide a list of key references on request. E-mail
     kenneth.anderson@ed.ac.uk.

The work in that term comprised three project cycles, each of which included an individual tutorial to discuss tutor feedback given on students' first drafts, following which they produced a revised, final draft. The first two projects were done collaboratively in groups, each student being asked to contribute one part of the text; the final project was done individually.

We collected data on the 10 students who completed the 11-week term. The majority were from countries in East Asia, but the group included individual students from the Middle East, North Africa, South America, and Southern Europe. Most were graduates intending to start postgraduate studies in the UK later in the year.

2. Research design

2.1 Research questions

1. What are AE students' attitudes to different types of feedback?
2. Do they change over time?
3. Which points are topicalised in written feedback, and in one-to-one tutorials?
4. Who topicalises them – student or tutor?
5. Does their writing show change (between drafts, but also from project to project) as a result of feedback?
6. If so, in which areas?

2.2 Method

We collected four kinds of data for our study.

Questionnaires

A questionnaire adapted from Leki (1991) was administered to investigate students' attitudes to feedback, at the beginning and end of their course: their feelings about the importance of errors in general, and about the relative importance of different kinds of errors; how often they looked carefully at comments in different areas, including content and organisation as well as language; and how they wanted the teacher to deal with errors.

Projects

We kept copies of both drafts of the learners' projects, to have a record of feedback given and changes made.

Tutorials

We recorded the one-to-one tutorials.

Assessment of texts

The first and final drafts of each text were graded (blind) by three native speakers.

3. Results

So far we have analysed the results for two students, 'Wendy' and 'Ahmed' – chosen because they were from very different backgrounds, linguistically and culturally, and in terms of sex, educational level, experience, and level of English.

'Ahmed', a Saudi mature postgraduate in his late twenties, had worked in management and was planning to start a master's course in October 2001. He had been at IALS since the previous October, and had made good progress; by the start of the term his proficiency level, had reached the equivalent of approximately 6.0 on the International English Language Testing System (IELTS). Tutors regarded him as a diligent and successful language student.

'Wendy', a Hong Kong Chinese newcomer to IALS, had lived in the UK for five years, having recently completed a mathematics degree at a Scottish university. In view of this, her English was surprisingly poor, with a placement score equivalent to below IELTS 4.5. In social interaction with her peers, she deployed very successful communication strategies, but the language she produced in speech and writing was very inaccurate; she showed signs of fossilisation.

3.1 Attitudes of AE students

First we analysed the questionnaires of all 10 students embarking on the AE course. The results are similar to Leki's (1991):

- Half thought it very important to minimise errors.
- Grammar and vocabulary were rated more highly than other areas; only three thought punctuation very important.
- However, a greater number said they 'always looked carefully' at marks referring to content and organisation than grammar; Leki also found this apparent mismatch between opinion and actual practice.
- Half said they wanted all errors indicated; the rest said either most major errors or just those interfering with communication.
- Locating the error and giving a clue was (as in Leki's study) more popular than supplying the correct form; but paradoxically, in Part 4, in which they were given sample actual feedback-types to judge, more preferred the correct form to be supplied.

As to whether their attitudes changed over the course, the findings regarding the two learners we focused on are summarised below:

Wendy	Ahmed
– *more* important than previously to have as few errors as possible (both for self and teacher) – punctuation increased in importance, to equal other categories – continued to look carefully at all indications of error – indications of linguistic error more important than previously – comments on organisation slightly less important – now more useful to consult teacher than grammar book – supplying correct form still preferred technique	– *more* important than previously to have as few errors as possible – grammatical errors still most important – now looked more carefully than before at indications of errors in grammar and spelling – continued always to look at comments on organisation and ideas – his preferred technique was still location of error and clue; preference stronger than previously

Table 1: Changes in the subjects' attitudes to feedback over the course

3.2 Which points are topicalised in written feedback, and in one-to-one tutorials?

Written feedback

We identified 50 types of 'points' selected by the tutor for written feedback in the texts written by Ahmed and Wendy, in four broad categories:

1.   Discourse (DIS) encompassed more global issues of text structure, and concerns such as plagiarism; this corresponds quite closely to Hyland's 'Academic' category (2001).

2.   Presentation (PRE) included errors of spelling, punctuation and word-processing, and issues of format in references, sub-headings, etc.
3.   Grammar (GRA) and
4.   Lexis (LEX) are self-explanatory (though the distinction is not straightforward).

Initiation of tutorial episodes

In analysing the tutorial recordings, we divided the discussion into topical 'episodes', the start of each episode being determined by a change of topic. We coded the episodes according to: the four topical categories above; whether the episode focused on a point in the tutor's written feedback (W) or not (NW); and whether it was initiated by the student or the tutor. There were striking differences between the tutorials with Ahmed and those with Wendy (Tables 2–5).

Ahmed used the tutorials in a different way from the others: he brought along a fully word-processed intermediate draft which he wanted the tutor to check, having already made revisions in the light of the written feedback.

As Tables 2–3 show, Ahmed's tutorials were characterised by a large number of topical episodes (between 20 and 30 in each), over 80 per cent of which were initiated by Ahmed himself. As the discussion was based on his revisions, almost all of the episodes were in the W category. Ahmed's interest was very clearly centred on issues of linguistic form, particularly the GRA and LEX topical categories. A larger number of episodes were classed as DIS in the third (individual) project, because his first draft had comprised the main body only, and he had supplied the missing elements (e.g., title page, introduction) in the redraft he presented at the tutorial.

W = discussion refers to written feedback point
NW = discussion does not refer to written feedback point

	Project 1			Project 2			Project 3			All projects		
Topic	W	NW	Total	W	NW	Total	W	NW	Total	W	NW	Total
DIS	1	0	1	0	1	1	7	0	7	8	1	9
GRA	9	0	9	16	0	16	8	0	8	33	0	33
LEX	3	0	3	5	0	5	4	0	4	12	0	12
PRE	1	0	1	3	1	4	4	1	5	8	2	10
All	14	0	14	24	2	26	23	1	25	61	3	64

Table 2: Ahmed: Tutorial episodes initiated by student

	Project 1			Project 2			Project 3			All projects		
Topic	W	NW	Total	W	NW	Total	W	NW	Total	W	NW	Total
DIS	0	0	0	0	0	0	0	0	0	0	0	0
GRA	2	0	2	0	1	1	2	0	2	4	1	5
LEX	1	2	3	0	0	0	1	0	1	2	2	4
PRE	0	1	1	1	0	1	2	0	2	3	1	4
All	3	3	6	1	1	2	5	0	5	9	4	13

Table 3: Ahmed: Tutorial episodes initiated by tutor

Ahmed was what teachers would regard as a 'good' student: he approached the task of revising methodically and carefully, and he used the tutorial in a focused, efficient way to elicit feedback on his formal corrections. By the same token, however, his approach arguably reflected a teacher-dependent mode of learning.

Tables 4 and 5 show a very different pattern for Wendy:

	Project 1			Project 2			Project 3			All projects		
Topic	W	NW	Total	W	NW	Total	W	NW	Total	W	NW	Total
DIS	1	2	3	2	1	3	0	0	0	3	3	6
GRA	0	0	0	0	0	0	3	0	3	3	0	3
LEX	1	0	1	0	0	0	6	0	6	7	0	7
PRE	0	0	0	0	2	2	1	0	1	1	2	3
All	2	2	4	2	3	5	10	0	10	14	5	19

Table 4: Wendy: Tutorial episodes initiated by student

	Project 1			Project 2			Project 3			All projects		
Topic	W	NW	Total	W	NW	Total	W	NW	Total	W	NW	Total
DIS	1	3	4	0	1	1	1	0	1	2	4	6
GRA	2	0	2	1	0	1	3	1	4	6	1	7
LEX	1	0	1	0	0	0	2	2	4	3	2	5
PRE	0	0	0	0	0	0	0	0	0	0	0	0
All	4	3	6	1	1	2	6	3	9	11	7	18

Table 5: Wendy: Tutorial episodes initiated by tutor

Firstly, there is a marked contrast between the figures for Wendy's first two tutorials and for the third; could this reflect a change in attitude? Her first two tutorials were very short (around five minutes), and comprised few episodes (10 and seven). The balance between student-initiated and tutor-initiated episodes was also much more equal. Interestingly, almost half of Wendy's questions were about points unrelated to the tutor's feedback (NW). Perhaps she did not see the written feedback as very relevant to her concerns; the points it focused on may have been in areas she was not 'ready' to address. In contrast to Ahmed, practically all Wendy's questions in the first two sessions were in the DIS category.

In the third tutorial, however, Wendy's behaviour had become more like Ahmed's. She had more questions, this time all relating to the tutor's feedback, and all in the GRA and LEX areas. Her shift in interest from 'higher order' concerns towards lexicogrammar runs counter to the direction that many EAP tutors would maintain is desirable. However, our analysis of the topics focused on by the tutor in feedback and in tutor-initiated tutorial episodes supports Hyland's finding of a mismatch between what EAP writing tutors may say are their priorities (higher-order 'academic' issues) and what they actually give most attention to in practice (grammar and vocabulary) (2001). It may be Wendy was learning to conform to what she had sensed to be the values of the institution – and, indeed, as a potentially 'fossilised' learner, this new attention to form may in her case be what she most needed.

The apparent change in Wendy's attitudes might also be interpreted as signalling increased dependence on the tutor, which would be consistent with her questionnaire responses (see Table 1). Given Wendy's hitherto rather unsuccessful record as a language learner, on the other hand, this newly acquired appreciation of the tutor's potential as a source of information on linguistic form may be encouraging: she may only now be entering a stage at which she is ready to 'notice the gap' between her interlanguage and the target language (Schmidt and Frota, 1986), when *Focus on Form* will pay off. An alternative, or additional, explanation might be an enhanced sense of personal commitment to the product, as it was an individual rather than a group project.

3.3 Students' writing: change over time

All three markers noted improvement, both between the first and final draft of each of Wendy and Ahmed's projects (suggesting they were taking up feedback effectively vis-à-vis the piece of work in question) and between the first and third projects (suggesting they were making progress in their writing during the course of the term).

To examine the learners' responses to feedback in more detail, we coded every instance of feedback in the first draft, and every instance of uptake in the second. The possible permutations are listed in the left-hand column of Table 6.

Italics = improvement in second draft

Categories of feedback and response	Number of instances per project % of all responses (% of responses to written feedback)					
	W1	W2	W3	A1	A2	A3
A: written feedback + discussed + improved	*3* *7%* *(9%)*	*3* *25%* *(43%)*	*15* *34%* *(42%)*	*17* *81%* *(89%)*	*21* *60%* *(66%)*	*28* *47%* *(52%)*
B: written feedback + discussed + changed but not improved	2 7% (9%)	1 8% (14%)	1 2% (3%)	0 0% (0%)	2 6% (6%)	1 2% (2%)
C: written feedback + discussed + not changed	1 4% (4%)	0 0% (0%)	0 0% (0%)	0 0% (0%)	0 0% (0%)	0 0% (0%)
D: written feedback + not discussed + improved	*10* *36%* *(43%)*	*2* *17%* *(29%)*	*16* *36%* *(44%)*	*1* *5%* *(5%)*	*7* *20%* *(22%)*	*19* *32%* *(35%)*
E: written feedback + not discussed + changed but not improved	1 4% (4%)	1 8% (14%)	3 7% (8%)	0 0% (0%)	1 3% (3%)	0 0% (0%)
F: written feedback + not discussed + not changed	6 21% (26%)	0 0% (0%)	1 2% (3%)	1 5% (5%)	1 3% (3%)	6 10% (11%)
G: no written feedback + not discussed + improved	*3* *11%*	*0* *0%*	*2* *5%*	*0* *0%*	*0* *0%*	*4* *7%*
H: no written feedback + not discussed + changed + not improved	0 0%	2 17%	3 7%	0 0%	0 0%	0 0%
I: no written feedback + discussed + improved	*1* *7%*	*3* *25%*	*2* *5%*	*2* *10%*	*2* *6%*	*1* *2%*
J: no written feedback + discussed + changed + not improved	1 4%	0 0%	0 0%	0 0%	1 3%	0 0%
K: no written feedback + discussed + not changed	0 0%	0 0%	1 2%	0 0%	0 0%	0 0%

Table 6: Responses to feedback in each of Wendy's and Ahmed's projects

Looking at response type A, it is clear that Ahmed produced considerably more responses of this type than Wendy, overall. However, Wendy's type A responses increased in number over the three projects, whereas Ahmed's decreased over the three projects in percentage terms, as his ability to act on written feedback alone (response type D) increased. Points raised in the tutorial only, and not mentioned in written feedback (types I, J, and K), almost always led to improvement.[2]

4. Conclusion

This preliminary study has underlined for us the sheer amount of work AE students put into the revision process, a major part of which necessarily entails attention to linguistic form, confirming that the feedback-revision cycle can be a highly productive context for *Focus on Form*. Secondly, the 'success rate' of the discussions has re-inforced our appreciation of the importance of one-to-one dialogue in this cycle. It has also highlighted the diversity of individual approaches to the tutorial, and the need for dialogue among students and tutor on how feedback can be provided and exploited (cf. Leki, 1991). We believe an extension of this research on a wider scale would be of value, and that the findings would be illuminated by finding out more about the students' previous experience in learning and using English, and about their attitudes to writing in their L1.

2   The issue of the relationship between who initiated the discussion of a point (the tutor or the student) and subsequent improvements to the text is discussed in a longer paper to appear in *Edinburgh Working Papers in Applied Linguistics*.

References

Hyland, F. 2001. 'Does teacher feedback make a difference?' Paper presented at BALEAP 2001 conference. *English for Academic Purposes: Directions for the Future.* Glasgow: University of Strathclyde.

Leki, I. 1991. 'The preferences of ESL students for error correction in college-level writing classes'. *Foreign Language Annals* 24/3, 203–218.

Long, M. 1991. 'Focus on form: A design feature in language teaching methodology'. In K. de Bot, C. Kramsch, and R. Ginsberg (eds.) *Foreign Language Research in Crosscultural Perspective.* Amsterdam: John Benjamins, 39–52.

Schmidt, R. and S. Frota. 1986. 'Developing basic conversational ability in a second language: a case study of an adult learner of Portuguese'. In R. Day (ed.) *Talking to Learn.* Rowley, Miss.: Newbury House, 237–326.

JOHNSON A. KALU
Writing: an assessment of students' learning outcomes

Introduction

It is a given among English Language Teaching practitioners that competence in written communication is essential for academic success (Blue, 1993; Swales, 1993), though the reality of the improvement realised via the provision of English for Academic Purposes (EAP) courses is often less than desired. At the University of Botswana, for example, anecdotal evidence from subject departments suggests student writing often does not seem to improve after these students have taken the communication skills course in their first year. This paper attempts to ascertain objectively to what extent such scepticism is justified.

Communication skills at the University of Botswana

The University of Botswana's Communication and Study Skills course is taken by all first-year students and aims at equipping them with communication skills essential for university study. The skills covered in the course include time management, essay and report writing, reading and oral presentation skills. A pass in the course is a graduation requirement.

Up until the 1999/2000 academic year, the course was run by the Department of English, and the teaching arrangement then was such that every academic member of the Department, irrespective of specialisation, was involved in the teaching. Prior to that year a number of stakeholders, including employers, sponsors, and content area lecturers, had expressed dissatisfaction with the performance of products of the course in expressive communication skills, leading the university to start exploring options for making the course more responsive to the needs of students and meeting the expectations of all parties that had interest in the course. The option taken by the university was the establishment of an independent unit, the Communication and Study Skills Unit (CSSU), which was charged with the responsibility of teaching and researching in the area of academic communication skills. The unit was to be staffed with specialists in EAP, English for Specific Purposes, and related fields. The unit took off in the 2000/2001 academic year with a mandate to make EAP courses outcomes-based, both in orientation and implementation.

Academic writing, the subject of this paper, is a skill, the acquisition of which can best be measured in terms of students' learning outcomes. In the context of teaching and learning, Spady defines outcomes as 'the learning results we desire from students that lead to culminating demonstrations' (1994). In other words, an outcomes-based approach prepares students to do and not just to know.

The need for educational reform in neighbouring South Africa has led to a wide acceptance of an outcomes-based educational philosophy. Sewlall describes this as a shift from 'content-based learning to an emphasis on the acquisition of skills' and highlights the devastating effect of traditional, content-based learning on university students:

> [...] the progressive lowering of standards in white education has created a body of students who have been exposed only to an authoritarian system which emphasises rote learning, and thus works against the nature of university study which demands the ability to work independently. (2000)

Sewlall's remark echoes the problem of students at the University of Botswana where the deleterious effects of rote learning on students are manifest in many ways, including their inability to think critically, learn independently, sustain an argument in speech and writing, make deductions and inferences, and distinguish fact from opinion. Plagiarism in students' writing is worrisome to both EAP and content area lecturers. As the CSSU maps out strategies for fulfilling its mandate, it is important that it takes a retrospective inventory of the circumstances that led to its establishment and harness lapses of years past as input for strategic planning and implementation of its academic programmes.

The data

The data for this study consist of 90 essay scripts written by the same group of students during their first and third years at the University of Botswana. The first 30 scripts were pre-course essays written by the students on their first lecture in communication skills. The next 30 scripts were first-year final examination essays while the third 30 scripts were third-year final examination essays. The three essay questions were as follows:

1.   First-year pre-course essay, 1997/98:

     Discuss the relevance of your course of study to the development of your country.

2.   First-year final examination essay, 1997/98:

     Compare and contrast traditional religion and Christianity.

3.   Third-year final examination essay, 1999/2000:

     The study of grammar serves no useful purpose. Do you agree? Support your stand with well-reasoned argument.

Method

Each of the scripts for the first and third years was marked, focusing on four categories: paragraphing, grammar, mechanics, and sentence quality. Each category was weighted 10 marks. The scripts were then paired after marking and the paired t-test was used to determine whether there was a significant improvement in both the four individual categories and in the overall writing performance.

Results

The results are presented in two tables. The first highlights the performance of students in the individual categories (paragraph, grammar, sentence quality, and mechanical skills) while the second presents the overall performance.

Pairs	Std. Error	95% Confidence Interval		t	df	Sign. (2-tld)
		Lower	Upper			
1. P0–P1	.1511	−1.5757	−9576	−8.382	29	.000
2. P1–P3	.1006	−.4057	5.695E–03	−1.989	29	.056
3. MS0–MS1	.3704	−3.9909	−2.4758	−8.729	29	.000
4. MS1–MS3	.1639	−.7685	−9.82E–02	−2.644	29	.013
5. G0–G1	9.767E–02	−.4998	−.1002	−3.071	29	.005
6. G1–G3	7.350E–02	−.2503	5.033E–02	−1.361	29	.184
7. SE0–SE1	.1000	−1.1045	−.6955	−9.000	29	.000
8. SE1–SE3	.1168	−.3055	.1722	−.571	29	.573

Table 1: Comparison of performance in individual writing categories.

Table 1 above shows a comparison of students' performance in the four individual writing categories. In the first pair (P0–P1), the performance of students in paragraph development in the pre-course test (P0) and in the first-year final examination in communication skills (P1) are compared. Results of the paired t-test indicate a significant improvement in students' paragraph development skills. In other words, students performed much better in paragraph development in the first year final examination than they did in the pre-course test. The second pair (P1–P3) compares the performance of students in the same skill (paragraph development) in their first-year (P1) final examination and in their third-year (P3) final examination. The result of this comparison shows there was no significant improvement in students' paragraph development skills between the two levels. The implication of this is that third-year students did not develop paragraphs better than they did in their first year in the university. The pattern for all the categories compared is that whereas performance in the first-year final examination shows a significant improvement over performance in the pre-course test, there is no significant improvement between students' performance in the first-year and third-year final examinations. The results indicate that in their third year, the students did not perform significantly better than they did in the first year in paragraph development, mechanical skills, grammar, and sentence quality. Table 2 shows the overall performance of students in essay writing.

Pairs	Std. Error	95% Confidence Interval		t	df	Sign. (2-tld)
		Lower	Upper			
1. T0–T1	.1511	−1.5757	−9576	−8.382	29	.000
2. T0–T3	.1006	−.4057	5.695E−03	−1.989	29	.056
3. T1–T3	.3704	−3.9909	−2.4758	−8.729	29	.000

Table 2: Overall performance in writing

The overall performance of students in the essays is compared in three pairs in Table 2. In the first pair, students' performance in the pre-course test (T0) and the first-year final examination (T1) are compared and the result shows that there was a significant improvement in the overall written communication skills of students. In the second pair, performance in the pre-course test (T0) was compared with performance in the third-year final examination (T3) and the result again shows a significant improvement in students' overall proficiency in essay writing. Finally, in the third pair, performances in the first-year and the third-year final examinations were compared and the result shows that there was no significant difference in the overall proficiency of students at this level. This result is in agreement with the findings in Table 1 and confirms our observation that students did not write significantly better in their third year than they did in the first year.

Discussion

The nature of academic writing problems observed in the scripts, in addition to my interview with course lecturers and scrutiny of materials and syllabi used in the course indicated a number of reasons for students' lack of proficiency in academic writing during the period (1997–1999) covered by this study. First, it appears there was a mismatch between teaching goals and learning outcomes. Course lecturers seemed more preoccupied with how much of the syllabus they covered than what students actually learnt from the course. The course was not outcomes-based, hence students' inability to demonstrate mastery of basic EAP writing skills. Secondly, the course syllabus was not based on an established academic writing needs.

Furthermore, the course was not task-based, so students' exposure to academic writing skills was not reinforced through independent and guided practice. In addition, the restriction of continuous assessment tests and final examinations to almost the same skill areas – essay writing, note making, and summary writing – limited students' ability to explore other academic writing genres.

The essays also show most of the students are incapable of transfer of learning. As a result, skills taught in the first year are not reflected in their writing in the third year in their specialist disciplines. This suggests students still engage in rote learning, even in the university. Besides, students' negative attitude to the English language in general and communication skills in particular is a demotivating factor which does not enhance learning. Finally, large communication skills classes at the University of Botswana make the teaching of skills almost impossible.

What follows is an illustration of students' weaknesses in the four categories (paragraphing, grammar, sentence quality, and mechanical skills) examined in this study.

1. Paragraphing

Most of the essays have paragraphs that are either poorly developed or not developed at all. The traditional qualities of a good paragraph – unity, coherence, and adequate development – are not reflected in most of the essays. In fact most of the introductory paragraphs read like opening statements in a high school debate, and some of them are very good illustrations of circular reasoning.

i. The study of grammar is a waste of time because it has no useful purpose. The above statement is not true because the study of grammar is not a waste of time and it has a very useful purpose

ii. 'The study of grammar is a waste of time because it has no useful purpose'. This statement is wholly or totally wrong. The writer of this essay is totally, without compromise, *agaist* this statement. The grammar of any language has to be studied.

iii. I think the statement which says the study of grammar is a waste of time and also that it has no purpose which is useful, is misleading and totally unfounded

iv. Grammar is the *prescribtive* and *describtive* study of rules of a particular language. The knowledge of such rules are important in the day to day communication in any society

v. There is what is called pure interest, that is the *accumilation* of knowledge of language just for the like of it. This pure *curiousity* of how language *work*. The study of grammar is of use because it *make* explicit the knowledge that the native speaker already had

2. Grammar

The following are some examples of grammatical deviations with high frequency in the students' essays:

a) Lack of concord

    i.   This broad definition enable us to study grammar
    ii.   Even though a native speaker has a linguistic competence they can still create ungrammatical sentences
    iii.   It makes explicit the knowledge that the native speaker already had
    iv.   Richard et al argues that grammar or language is a system of communication
    v.   This type of grammar include the basic sounds
    vi.   This take into account the language use and appropriateness
    vii.   The study of grammar will also take into account language learning which Leech and Svartvik has termed the acquisition of competencies
    viii.   The above *definitious* of grammar talks of it as a component [...]
    ix.   Studying phonetics help with the pronunciation
    x.   I am against the statement which say 'The study of grammar is a waste of time'

b) Inappropriate lexical choice

There are many instances in the essays where intended meaning is blurred by wrong choice of word:

    i.   The study of grammar avoids some confusions
    ii.   Scientists of grammar can study grammar focusing on its structure
    iii.   An example of a *grammarist* is Aitchison
    iv.   Grammar is very important since it is the study of rules and regulations governing the use of a language
    v.   By setting up rules and regulations which the speakers abide by will eradicate the problem of new *eventions*
    vi.   Language study is not a waste of time since language analysis is one of the *perculiarities* for solving the problem of brain damage
    vii.   Grammar has been fragmented or subdivided into sects.

c) Intrusion and deletion of articles

    i. Studying phonetics help with <u>the</u> pronunciation
    ii. Some study grammar because they want to teach it to <u>the</u> foreigners
    iii. For one to be able to teach (–) grammar of a particular language, he has to know the structure of that language.
    iv. We need to study (–) grammar of our language so that we can understand how the grammar of other languages behave.

3. Sentence quality

In terms of sentence quality, the most prominent problem observed is wordiness and this rendered most of the sentences incoherent because of the high incidence of redundancies as illustrated by the following:

    i. I personally negate this statement because it does not make any sound reason but it is dismissive or it is a sweeping statement.
    ii. On another note the study of grammar is very essential because it shows or help us know what certain sounds in some languages comes before others in the constructions of language sentences.
    iii. In conclusion, as I have stated at the beginning of the essay I still maintain my argument that grammar is very essential to us because it is the controlling factor to us to understand language.
    iv. I have in mind here of people who have studied grammar and because of their knowledge will help or contribute towards the development of their country by helping or teaching foreigners or those who need to learn their language for various purposes.
    v. The students of *linguistic* learn about language, they do not learn language so for one to be able to teach grammar of a particular language he has to know the structure of that language and be up to date with the researches of that language.
    vi. As already mentioned there are many definitions concerning as to what grammar but all these definitions come to one thing that grammar of a language.
    vii. When we take the definition of Rodman and Fromkin we see that they define grammar as the linguistic competence of a language by a native speaker of that particular language.

4. Mechanics (spelling, punctuation, capitalisation)

    i. Grammar should include the study of the vocabulary
    ii. Similarly in relation to grammar this method has been applicable in a number of ways.
    iii. It is imperative, to study grammar because, we get to learn a lot of things about our language.
    iv. Language is a broad, issue, and grammar is part of it.
    v. The study of grammar is not a waste of time, it is vital in our lives.
    vi. Language is a system of Communication.
    vii. I definately do not agree with the statement.
    viii. Prescribtive grammar helps one in improving language.
    ix. Grammer has been defined differently by scholars.
    x. Grammar has proverbs and ideoms.

The numerous examples of the writing problems of third-year students revealed by this study suggest there are significant deficiencies to be addressed, especially in the areas of instructional methodology, course and syllabus design and students' learning strategies.

Conclusion

This paper set out to assess the learning outcomes of third-year university students in academic writing skills. Results of the study show that students' writing skills in the third year (just one year before graduation) do not differ significantly from the skills they had acquired at the close of the first year. The poor writing skills of our third-year students is deeply unsettling given the fact that in just one year most of them will graduate and gain employment. For graduates who will be employed as teachers in high schools, for instance, we can only imagine the type of basic writing skills they would impart to their students. The cycle of training students 'to communicate poorly' continues. It is therefore recommended that the newly established Communication and Study Skills Unit should reorganise its EAP writing programme such that it is outcomes- or performance-based in design and implementation, it is based on established needs analysis that takes into account the interest of all stake holders in the programme, and that it is responsive to both immediate and target situation needs.

References

Blue, G. 1993. 'Nothing succeeds like linguistic competence: the role of language in academic success'. In G. Blue *Language, Learning and Success: Studying through English.* London: Macmillan, 4–13.

Jordan, R. 1997. *English for Academic Purposes: A Guide and Resource Book for Teachers.* Cambridge: Cambridge University Press.

Sewlall, H. 2000. 'English at the turn of the millennium: reflections on undergraduate literary studies in an OBE paradigm'. *Journal for Language Teaching* 34/2, 170–179.

Spady, W. 1994. *Outcomes-Based Education – Critical Issues and Answers.* Arlington: The American Association of School Administrators.

Swales, J. 1990. *Genre Analysis.* Cambridge: Cambridge University Press.

SIÂN PREECE

Language and identity issues with *home* students on EAP writing programmes at the University of Westminster

Introduction

In British higher education there is, increasingly, a new (but as yet largely uncharted) set of pedagogical challenges coming to the professional forefront: developing EAP (English for Academic Purposes) with students who are conversant with English-speaking cultural contexts and use everyday and colloquial English with ease, but seem far less familiar with the ethos and language of higher education. These learners are generally classed as *home* students and many have been educated solely within the British education system. This article seeks to raise this issue as one needing debate in EAP, both on a theoretical level and as a teaching issue.

Context

The University of Westminster has an ethnically diverse student population. According to the *Student Access, Academic Achievement and First Destinations Report* (2000), 46.6 per cent of the University's *home* students were from ethnic minority groups in 1996/7 compared to the national average of 12.8 per cent.[1] In the current academic year, this figure has risen to 49.4 per cent.[2] Many of these students have

---

1   Based on HESA statistics.
2   Based on student self-reporting collected by Admissions.

been routinely categorised as *bilingual* learners by the British education system because of the use of other languages, in addition to English, in their homes and communities. Although bilingualism has been the focus of much debate in British education,[3] Leung, Harris, and Rampton (1997); Harris (1997, 1998); and Rampton (1990, 1995) have recently taken a critical stance on this issue contrasting a prevalent and *over-romanticised* view of bilingualism with the 'everyday linguistic, ethnic and cultural experiences of "bilingual learners"' (Harris, 1997).

Since bilingual learners with a similar profile to those involved in Leung, Harris, and Rampton's research are entering universities such as Westminster, a variety of issues have become pertinent to those of us who encounter these students on EAP/academic writing pro-grammes. One of these is the notion of the *native speaker,* which has been the subject of a long-standing debate in the English Language Teaching profession. Various cultural theorists have argued that notions of a homogeneous British society speaking a standardised form of the language have consistently reinforced images of people from ethnic minorities as outsiders to *mainstream* society.[4] Leung, Harris and Rampton comment that there has to be a point at which settled migrant groups are regarded as a 'permanent and integral part of the host nation' (1997).

Rather than focusing on *native speakers*, it is my contention that we should adopt Rampton's constructs of language *expertise,* language *affiliation,* and language *inheritance* (1990). In other words, the questions of: (1) what we know about our students' expertise in the varieties of English they use, the languages they use at home and the foreign languages they learn at school; (2) what we know about our students' sense of affiliation to these languages; and (3) whether there is an automatic link between belonging to an ethnic group and inheriting its language (Leung, Harris, and Rampton, 1997). In my view, it is crucial for those of us working with *home* students on EAP

3   See, e.g., Bullock (1975), Swann (1985), OFSTED (1994)
4   Unfortunately, space does not permit a full exploration of this issue. However, heated debates concerning British national identity are currently very much to the fore in the political and press arenas and we should not consider ourselves immune or isolated from these issues in our role as educators.

courses to enrich our understanding of these issues in order to develop a pedagogy which can facilitate these students' taking up academic voice and developing academic identity in higher education.

In order to shed light on these complexities, some initial research was conducted with students registered on a Written Communication Skills (WCS) module at the University of Westminster. The majority of the students were first year full-time undergraduates registered at the Westminster Business School (WBS). It is worth noting that all first-year WBS students had taken an *Assessment of Written Academic Literacy* (AWAL)[5] on entry to the university. *Home* students receiving low scores in this test were then obliged to enrol for the WCS programme.

To date research has been conducted in two phases. Firstly, groups of students were asked to record a discussion on the theme of language and identity, then complete a questionnaire based on the issues raised in their discussions. The questionnaire data[6] showed a total of 21 languages were used at home including English. After English, Asian languages accounted for the largest number of speakers with 26 students speaking Punjabi, Gujarati, or Urdu and nine students speaking Hindi, Tamil, Bengali, Cantonese, or Vietnamese. There were also a number of students reporting the use of African languages, such as Ghanaian, Kamba, Swahili, and Yoruba.

It appears, therefore, that the AWAL is picking up students traditionally categorised as bilingual learners. The majority of these at Westminster are British Asian students with a smaller, but substantial, number of Black African students, who are generally mature students studying part-time. While the British Asian students have had all or most of their compulsory education in Britain, the African students have usually been educated in English outside Britain. At present there are very few students traditionally classed as monolingual English speakers on the course, which raises the question of whether the WBS is attracting fewer non-traditional White or Black British students and/or whether these students are more conversant with academic English and are therefore receiving higher scores in the

---

5   A placement test devised by EAP lecturers at the University of Westminster.
6   Note that there were 43 responses, which represents roughly 50 per cent of the students registered on the module for the current semester.

AWAL. It is worth noting, however, two conclusions from the *Student Access Report* (2000) in connection with this. Firstly, the suggestion that White and Black Caribbean[7] students from lower social class groups[8] are currently underrepresented at the university and secondly, the worrying finding that Black students[9] were generally much less likely to receive a first class or upper second class degree from the university. Although it is outside the scope of this paper to explore these issues further, they are clearly areas for further investigation.

Research findings

A closer analysis of the situations in which the WCS students use their *home* languages reveals their use is restricted primarily to the family, particularly those family members representing the *home* culture, as the following examples illustrate:

> When I speak to my parents or elder generation relatives I speak Bengali. However, when I speak to my sisters and friends I speak English, unless I cannot explain something without speaking Bengali.

> I use Vietnamese to communicate mainly with my parents or relatives at home. I use English to communicate at university, at home, with my friends, my lecturers or teachers, socialising.

> All the time [English]. Punjabi I only speak with my grandparents. Urdu is spoken with my parents only. I use English in almost every situation, in my studies, at work, and at home.

---

7   Note that the report used the 1991 Census categories and merged Black Other with Black Caribbean on the basis that many Black Other respondents were born in Britain but their 'home' culture is Caribbean.

8   Note that the Report used the UCAS application form response for the occupation of the person with the highest household income to determine this, which only one-third of students in the survey had answered.

9   The report classified Black Caribbean, Black African, and Black Other as one group for this section.

In all cases, English was the preferred language with siblings and friends, as well as for socialising, studying, working, and other everyday activities. In fact, as Fig. 1 shows, there was a noticeable difference between the numbers of *monolingual* English speakers in the home environment compared with friends. Four students reported using monolingual English at home, whereas this number rose to 27 with friends. The same contrast was discernible for settings in which other languages were used in preference to English. Fourteen students reported not speaking any English at home while all the students spoke English with friends. There seemed to be more equality between code switching in the different environments, with 25 reporting this at home and 16 with friends.

Language Use	At home	With friends
English only	4	27
Other language(s) only	14	0
Other language(s) and English	25	16

Figure 1: Language Use at Home and with Friends

It is necessary, however, to approach the results cautiously, particularly for students claiming not to use any English at home. Some of the students may either not be aware of code switching, or the nature of the questions may have lead to this answer. It is possible that by contrasting language use at *home* with language use with *friends*, students interpreted *home* primarily as the language used with their parents.

Although a diversity of *home* languages were reported by the students, we should exercise care about constructing a strong link between this 'inheritance' and an attachment to a particular language and culture. Leung, Harris, and Rampton argue many educational practices have tended to assume bilingual students have a strong attachment to the languages and culture of their homes and communities (1997). Their research into bilingual learners in London schools shows misleading assumptions have consequently been made about British bilingual students and that this has had implications for language pedagogy.

A preliminary analysis of the recorded data showed the emergence of varying degrees of affiliation to English, other *home* languages and different cultures as is illustrated in the following extracts in which three students, Dina, Maha, and Rose,[10] are discussing the question of identity.

Extract 1:

Maha: That's another reason why I'm not so– I'm more Westernised than, er–

Rose: Moroccan.

Maha: Yeah. I mean even though my [unclear section] my religion and my culture but the way I put them I'm more westernised than, you know–

Rose: More westernised.

Maha: Compared to my mum and dad, most definitely, and my brother.

Dina: You know– you know–

Rose: So you consider yourself Western?

Maha: I consider myself as, er, British.

Rose: British yeah. Mind you, you were born here so you are.

Maha: And Moroccan. I do consider myself–

Dina: Originate from Morocco but you're British.

Maha: Yeah, but I'm a British person, yeah most definitely, and an Arab.

In this exchange Maha gives the impression of mixed affiliations. She contrasts her notions of religion and culture with her parents and brother noting she has developed a merged Western and Arabic view. Despite identifying herself as British, rather than a generic Westerner, she immediately tempers this by adding her Moroccan origins. She then reaffirms this fusion by her statement that she is *definitely* British *and* an Arab. Maha's notion of drawing on different and diverse

---

10 Dina is British Asian, Maha is British Arab and both have done all schooling in Britain while Rose is an African student who came to Britain when she was 19. Note these are pseudonyms.

cultural traditions is in marked contrast to the way Rose views herself as exemplified in the following extract:

Extract 2:

Maha: We're just talking on. What about you like, what do you consider yourself as?

Rose: Kenyan.

Maha: Kenyan.

Rose: Yes.

Maha: Fully?

Rose: Fully Kenyan.

Dina: How long have you been living in this country for?

Rose: I've been here 11 years. I've got a British passport but I'm still Kenyan.

Maha: You don't consider yourself–

Rose: I consider myself as completely Kenyan.

Maha: At all, no British?

Rose: No.

This exchange continues with Maha and Dina pressing Rose on the subject of her strong identification with Kenya. However, Rose remains emphatic about her strong Kenyan affiliations and her lack of attachment to Britain. Maha and Dina's eventual conclusion is that their difference in outlook can be explained by their country of birth revealing their awareness that despite parental origins, the country in which children are raised and educated exerts a tremendous force on shaping identity.

Throughout the data, Maha demonstrates a sense of 'otherness', not about Britain and English, but about her *home* language, country, and culture although a relationship exists. A similar tendency also emerges from the other British students who have experienced all or the majority of their compulsory schooling in Britain. On the other hand, Rose still feels a tremendous sense of 'otherness' towards

Britain despite having British citizenship and being a resident in Britain for 11 years. In this sense she is typical of other mature African students who came to Britain as young adults, many of whom seem to associate English with formality and authority as the following comment illustrates:

> I never feel comfortable speaking in English with my family/friends because I always feel I am in a formal setting/environment.

The reasons for these perceptions are clearly complex. Sociologists such as Hall explain this phenomenon by arguing that instead of viewing identity as fixed and immutable, it should be viewed as both constructed and represented in historical, cultural. and political discourses(1988, 1992). In this sense, identity is unstable, fluid, and open to reconstruction. Hall discusses a movement away from notions of an essentialist British national identity towards a fusion of 'Britishness' with a variety of affiliations to form 'cultures of hybridity'. Hall equates the emergence of these new cultural identities with 'translation', the formation of a complex, hybrid identity, as opposed to 'tradition', the striving for ethnic purity and certainty, and 'assimilation', the replacement of a 'weaker' culture with a dominant one. As Hall notes:

> [People who are 'translated'] bear upon them the traces of the particular cultures, traditions, languages and histories by which they were shaped. The difference is that they are not and will never be *unified* in the old sense, because they are irrevocably the product of several interlocking histories and cultures, belong at one and the same time to several 'homes' (and to no one particular 'home'). People belonging to [...] *cultures of hybridity* have had to renounce the dream or ambition of rediscovering any kind of 'lost' cultural purity, or ethnic absolutism. They are irrevocably *translated* [...]. They are the products of the new *diasporas* created by the post-colonial migrations. They must learn to inhabit new identities, to speak two cultural languages, to translate and negotiate between them. (1992)

There is, moreover, an issue about the varieties of English to which these students are affiliated and whether these will be empowering in the academic community. While teaching the WCS students, I noticed the classroom was alive with 'London English' expressions such as *innit,* which peppered all of the students' speech.

Much of the data also revealed the way in which students con-
ceptualised varieties of English as the following comments illustrate:

> Do you speak the *proper* language?
> It's quite *slangy* the way I speak.
> If I talked to a *posh person*, I actually *spoke posh* with them.
> If you had *good* English, you'd get A's just like that.
> You know foreigners who learn English; *they speak better* English than us.

As can be seen the students tended to juxtapose terms such as,
proper and *posh* with *slangy*. Their comments and terminology
showed they were aware of the status of varieties of English and the
benefits of being able to utilise more high-status varieties in
educational settings. Furthermore, some of the data from the students
educated in Britain revealed an underlying tension based on the
perception that 'foreigners' had more access to high status varieties of
English through their education than students educated within the
British state system.

The use of non-standard English by the WCS students is perhaps
not surprising given the variety of sociolinguistic research which has
pointed out problems with assuming that British children routinely use
standard English. Hudson and Holmes, for example, conducted a
survey of the use of standard spoken English with 11- and 16-year
olds in Merseyside, Tyneside, London, and South West England
(1995). They suggest that a minority of British school students are
habitual speakers of standard English and that a gravitation towards
non-standard English may become even more marked as children
become older, despite exposure to standard English in school. This
accords with other sociolinguistic research over several decades that
has studied links between language use and communities or social
'networks' (Labov, 1972; Milroy, 1980; Cheshire, 1982, to name a
few). Much of this has concluded that vernacular forms of the
language are used to build group identity. The impact of contemporary
urban environments on language usage continues to be the focus of
research with Leung, Harris, and Rampton noting that many British
bilingual students are probably 'most comfortable linguistically with
[...] a local urban spoken English vernacular' (1997). One of the
questions for us is the way in which we can enable these students to

develop both affiliation and expertise with the more unfamiliar language and discourses of higher education.

These findings present us with new and different challenges than we have traditionally faced with international students, and raise the question of developing an EAP pedagogy which both accommodates and builds on the complex identities, language expertise and affiliations of our students. Further discussions are also needed on ways in which we can enable these students to move towards developing an academic identity and taking up voice in academic communities. In order to have this debate, we will need to look not only at the field of linguistics, but beyond into the wider arena of education.

References

Bullock Report. 1975. *A Language for Life*. London: HMSO.
Cheshire, J. 1982. 'Linguistic variation and social function'. In S. Romaine (ed.) *Sociolinguistic Variation in Speech Communities*. London: Edward Arnold, 153–166.
Education, Training and the Labour Market Research Group (2000). *Student Access, Academic Achievement and First Destinations at the University of Westminster*. Westminster Business School, University of Westminster: Unpublished report.
Hall, S. 1988. 'New ethnicities'. In A. Rattansi and J. Donald (eds.) *'Race', Culture and Difference*. London: Sage / Open University, 252–259.
Hall, S. 1992. 'The question of cultural identity'. In S. Hall, D. Held, and T. McGrew (eds.) *Modernity and its Futures*. Cambridge: Polity Press / Open University, 274–316.
Hall, S., D. Held, and T. McGrew (eds.). 1992. *Modernity and its Futures*. Cambridge: Polity Press / Open University.
Harris, R. 1997. 'Romantic bilingualism: time for a change?'. In C. Leung and C. Cable (eds.) *English as an Additional Language: Changing Perspectives*. Watford: NALDIC, 14–27.

Hudson, R. and J. Holmes. 1995. *Children's Use of Spoken Standard English*. London: School Curriculum and Assessment Authority.

Labov, W. 1972. *Language in the Inner City*. Oxford: Blackwell.

Leung, C. and C. Cable (eds.). 1997. *English as an Additional Language: Changing Perspectives*. Watford: NALDIC.

Leung, C., R. Harris, and B. Rampton. 1997. 'The idealised native-speaker, reified ethnicities and classroom realities'. *TESOL Quarterly* 31/3, 545–560.

Milroy, L. 1980. *Language and Social Networks*. Oxford: Blackwell.

Milroy, L. 1982. 'Social network and linguistic focusing'. In S. Romaine (ed.) *Sociolinguistic Variation in Speech Communities*. London: Edward Arnold, 141–152.

OFSTED. 1994. *Educational Support for Minority Ethnic Communities*. London: Office for Standards in Education.

Rampton, B. 1990. 'Displacing the "native speaker": expertise, affiliation and inheritance'. *ELT Journal* 44/2, 97–101.

Rampton, B. 1995. *Crossing: Language and Ethnicity among Adolescents*. London: Longman.

Rattansi, A. and J. Donald (eds.). 1988. *'Race', Culture and Difference*. London: Sage / Open University.

Romaine, S. (ed.). 1982. *Sociolinguistic Variation in Speech Communities*. London: Edward Arnold.

Swann Report. 1985. *Education for All*. London: HMSO.

Section 5:
Testing and Evaluation

IRENE TURNER, VAL GODWIN, AND LYNDA WILKS
A measure of success: changes in vocabulary usage on intensive EFL courses

Introduction

Communicative competence is an umbrella term for a whole raft of desirable features, but includes the ability to use appropriate vocabulary for effective communication in a range of social situations, and this is clearly one of the targets that language students and teachers aspire to. However, measuring competence levels for feedback to students, either formally in examinations, or as a measure of their success at the end of a language course, remains imprecise.

This paper reports an attempt to use a more precise measure in evaluating the progress made by students in developing their speaking skills on an intensive English course. The measuring instrument focuses, in particular, on the use of low frequency vocabulary in speech.

Background

Teachers and examiners look at a number of factors when they try to assess progress and proficiency in oral skills. These include the ability to discuss, describe, and speculate; comprehensibility and fluency; grammatical accuracy; cohesion; and vocabulary usage.

There seems good reason to think that vocabulary usage is an area of language which can be measured and, therefore, more accurately assessed. The criteria by which exams such as International English Language Testing Service (IELTS) and Cambridge FCE,

CAE, and CPE assess a learner's spoken performance include references to the type of vocabulary used at the different levels of ability. Thus the use of 'mundane' or simple vocabulary is linked with lower grades. 'Mundane' vocabulary seems inextricably associated with the use of high frequency words. At the higher levels it is expected that sophisticated or academic, i.e., infrequent vocabulary items, are used. 'Rising above the mundane' is an expression used in one set of criteria. We are not aware of research that attempts to link the use of infrequent vocabulary with improved speaking skills. However, Laufer and Nation's *Lexical Frequency Profile* (1995) makes exactly this link with improvement in writing skills. It seems reasonable to assume that if this can be applied to writing then it may also apply to speaking skills. The availability to us of a new vocabulary profiling program, PLex (Meara, 1998), offered the possibility of examining the issue in our centre.

The spoken data examined were collected during paired discussions in order to obtain our students' authentic spoken text. Paired discussions are often used in classrooms for practice and in examinations for assessment with either the examiner or another student taking the second pair part. While this technique is widely used as a means of eliciting language for making an assessment of language level, it is not certain this technique provides genuinely useful data, at least as far as vocabulary is concerned. Labov asserts that the most regular conversational style is the vernacular, and that the least attention is paid to speech in this style (1972). True, his attention was focused on the care given to pronunciation rather than vocabulary, but it seems reasonable to link the vernacular with the use of higher frequency vocabulary ranges. Paired classroom discussion has clear links with the features of everyday conversation. This may also hold true for paired discussions in examinations. The vocabulary used might, therefore, contain a high number of high frequency lexical items irrespective of the topic under discussion. A more formal speaking context might cause speakers to produce lower frequency, more 'difficult' words, as they are likely to be paying more attention to their speech.

In addition, the student's language options will be influenced by a desire to cooperate in the discussion. The interaction between social and psychological factors may affect the relative formality of the language the student chooses for his/her communicative purpose. If the speech event is perceived as relatively informal then the student may code-switch into a speaking style that pays less attention to formal vocabulary use and more attention to supporting the other conversation participant by accommodating their speech pattern. This may affect choice of language code in groups and individuals. Milroy observed that relationships between people in working class communities were reinforced by their use of the vernacular rather than prestige forms (1980, 1987).

Bell links the social situation the speaker is in with the linguistic choices the speaker makes (1984). In other words, speakers may change the way they speak and sound in order to be less like themselves and more like the person they are talking to. This is clearly relevant to language learners in discussion pairs either in classrooms or examinations who may adjust their language code in order to accommodate better to each other. Beebe and Giles note that convergence with another's speech patterns is powered by the pull factor of approval (1984). From this we might extrapolate that using low frequency vocabulary items which are at possible variance with another language learner's vocabulary knowledge is likely to inhibit rather than facilitate communication. In this case the use of less mundane, more unusual vocabulary should not be considered as indicative of better oral proficiency. Rather, in this instance it would indicate a student's communicative competence in adjusting to context and situation.

While the use of formal and infrequent vocabulary as a feature of spoken language use is an explicitly stated criterion for recognising able learners in spoken examinations, there seems some reason for thinking the common examination task type, the paired interview, may not actually elicit this type of language.

Method

Eight students attending a 10-week General and Academic English course were put into pairs of similar English language level, ranging from elementary, through intermediate, to advanced. Prompt sheets were given to the student pairs to guide them into developing question and response discussions based on information about their own countries (see Appendix). Care was taken to ensure each pair consisted of students of different nationality so that the task would be as valid as possible with the maximum information gap. The students' abilities ranged from elementary to advanced.

The student pairs were then sent to different rooms and the resulting question-and-answer dialogues were taped. No teacher was present so that the students could engage in free conversation. It appears the use of tape recorders in no way inhibited the discussions.

The first recording was made during the first week of a 10-week intensive English course. The whole process was then repeated in the final week of the course using the same students, but different pairs, though the original selection criteria (different nationality and similar English language level) were used. Again, the discussions focused on the students' countries. Approximately 15 minutes of each student's discourse from the week one and week 10 recordings were then transcribed.

As a control, an additional recording was made of a dialogue between a native speaker of English and a bilingual overseas research assistant, using the same prompt sheet. This recording was then transcribed.

Each transcript was analysed using PLex which is a lexical profiling system.

The PLex program

This is a program, developed by Paul Meara (University of Wales, Swansea), which works under Windows 95, and includes a set of dictionary files needed to work the programme. It is used to assess the difficulty of texts. It aims to improve on current methods of measuring lexical difficulty, particularly in shorter texts.

How PLex works

When a text is loaded into PLex, it is divided into segments of 10 words each. The PLex program analyses each block of text and divides the lexis it encounters into a number of files:

- the 50 most frequent structure/function (basic) words;
- 1000 most 'frequent' (easy) words;
- names and numbers; and
- hard words – a list of words recognised by PLex which are not in the other three groups.

The programme then counts the number of 'hard' words in each segment. Once it has classified the words occurring in the text, PLex constructs a profile of the text which shows the proportion of 10-word segments containing difficult words, the proportion containing one difficult word, the proportion containing two difficult words, and so on up to 10. Thus, following the analysis, a profile is produced as in Fig. 1.

PLex uses Poisson distributions (a probability density function used to calculate the likelihood of unrelated events), generated from a mathematical formula, the key value of which is lambda. It produces the theoretical Poisson curve which most closely matches the actual data produced from the text. Lambda values have a limited range, and are the final scores produced by PLex to represent the level of difficulty in the text. The higher the value lambda, the more likelihood words, and so the more difficult and lexically rich the text. In our

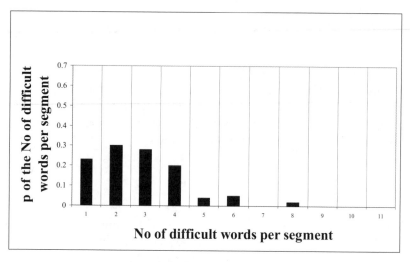

Figure 1

project, a high score was above 1.5. To give you an idea of what this means, the lambda score of Macbeth's soliloquy, 'Tomorrow, and tomorrow, and tomorrow…' has a lambda score of 2.66.

Once PLex has completed the lexical analysis of the text, it produces a report which consists of a number of statistics and a graph showing the distribution of the different words it has identified (Fig. 2).

Results

The results of the control pair will give a base line against which to compare the performance of the non-native speakers. Both subjects scored an identical lambda figure of 0.95. This is a low score when compared to the lambda scores gained from written texts. The PLex graph for the native speaker is shown is Fig. 3.

The results for the non-native speakers are also low compared to written text but are comparable with the control pair's scores. The pre- and post-test scores are shown in Fig. 4. It was felt the spoken English

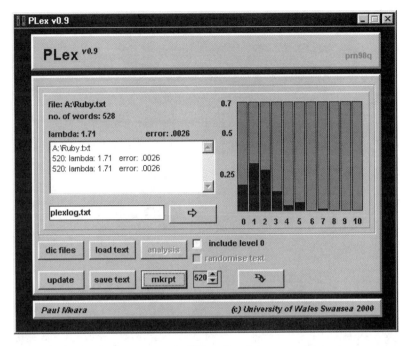

Figure 2

of every student had improved during the course of their instruction but this improvement does not seem to be reflected in the results gained from this analysis. These showed the opposite trend to that which would normally be expected or desirable if the examination criteria for assessing speech were to be applied. In most cases, (five out of eight), the lambda value of the second PLex analysis (week 10) was lower than that of the first (week one). The three students whose second lambda value had increased showed only a slight improvement. In addition, the lambda scores showed that sophistication of vocabulary used by higher and lower level students of English did not reflect their language level. The lower level students were in some cases using more sophisticated vocabulary in the transcripts analysed than higher level students, even though their fluency and communicative competence were far more limited.

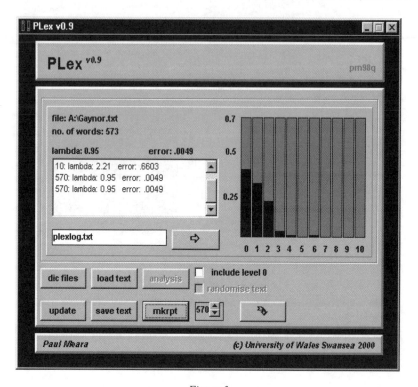

Figure 3

Students listed in approx. order of ability from highest to lowest[1]	Lambda value week 1	Lambda value week 10
1	0.31	0.36
2	1.71	0.84
3	0.74	0.53
4	1.09	0.61
5	0.80	1.03
6	0.69	0.59
7	0.32	0.57
8	1.04	0.66

Figure 4

1   The first four students were in a higher level English class and the second four had been placed in a lower level class, based on an entrance test.

Student 1, week 1

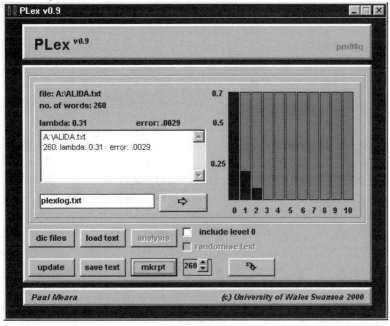

Figure 5

Fig. 5 shows an advanced level student using almost exclusively simple and highly frequent vocabulary during the course of this exercise. Compare this with Fig. 6 which shows a lower level student who manages to use more infrequent vocabulary in his speech.

Discussion

Because examination criteria link higher grades with the use of infrequent vocabulary items, it was expected our students would show improvement in this area at the end of the 10-week period. However, our results do not indicate an improvement in most of the subjects. Clearly, this raises the question of why this should be so.

Irene Turner, Val Godwin, and Lynda Wilks

Student 6, week 1

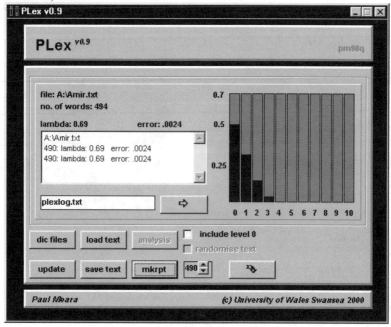

Figure 6

Two potential problem areas can, we think, be excluded. The small number of testees, for example, does not appear to be a factor. Small numbers in a sample may mean that you get odd students giving untypical results. However, we did not feel this was the case here.

Neither did we feel there was a problem with the method of analysis. The lexical profiling system is a well-established tool for measuring the number of 'hard' or statistically unusual words in a text.

It appears the answer may lie in the kind of task we asked our students to perform. It seems likely to us the task type really required and precipitated the use of a lot of informal language and hence highly frequent vocabulary. The fact that our control pair produced very similar profiles to those of the NNS subjects backs up this idea. This shows paired discussion and the kinds of general topics often used in English lessons and formal examinations may not elicit the level of vocabulary sophistication which is often considered to be an indication of language proficiency.

A number of questions naturally arise from this. Firstly, what part does use of sophisticated lexis play in interaction between native speakers? Native speaker competence includes knowing when to use 'hard' words and when to use high frequency words, and this was demonstrated by the control pair, who used high-frequency lexis, well suited to the task. As students progress in their language proficiency, we surely expect to see a move towards NS competence, with growing control over a wider range of vocabulary choices. Outside of an examination, a student's progress will largely be judged by how 'native' he or she sounds, and this will include use of vocabulary appropriate to the situation.

The second question is that of how oral examination candidates are graded. This seems to be done partly on appropriacy, but also on the sophistication of vocabulary used, even if the task does not naturally lend itself to the use of low frequency lexis. The current marking criteria may lead to candidates being downgraded if their vocabulary can be described as 'simple' or 'mundane'.

Thirdly, we must ask ourselves whether pair work itself automatically leads to the use of high frequency vocabulary and paraphrase because communication, rather than lexical sophistication, is the prime objective. The relationship between the pair of subjects should also be considered. In our study, the students were much more familiar with each other at the end of the 10-week period, and this could well have been a factor in their choice of language

We also need to take into account the apparent drop in the overall level of lexical sophistication in many students at both high and low levels. It has been suggested that learners tend to use a limited range of vocabulary in the very early stages of acquiring a language – perhaps knowing only one word to express a certain idea – and then begin to use more high frequency words as their communicative skills and knowledge of structures develop. Further, there must come a point for more advanced learners where they can choose what vocabulary to use, high or low frequency, according to the circumstances (J. Milton, personal communication; Fig. 7).

Another point which came out of this study is that during an examination, the assessor is effectively required to make quick judge-

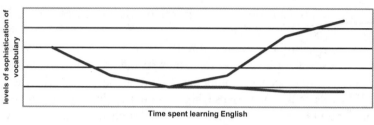

Time spent learning English

Figure 7

ments about whether certain words used by the candidate are high or low frequency. While we were running the transcripts through the PLex programme, we were surprised by how often our own intuition in this matter was wrong, and it would therefore seem unreasonable to expect oral examiners to be able to do some kind of accurate running lexical analysis on their candidates. It seems to us that the main issue raised by this project is the suitability of task type. Generally speaking, in a number of oral examinations, there is no objective way of saying whether the task type demands 'hard' or 'easy' vocabulary items. The band descriptors concerned with lexical sophistication may, therefore, be inappropriate.

Conclusion

A number of different features of spoken English are used in assessment of oral proficiency, for example, fluency, grammatical range and accuracy, pronunciation, and vocabulary resource. It is clear from assessment criteria that in the latter area, formal EFL/EAP examinations clearly expect an increase in levels of lexical sophistication to indicate ability. However, it would seem an increase in the level of sophistication of vocabulary is not a reliable, objective measure of the development of oral skills where the task type, namely the oral pair work exercise, does not require great lexical sophistication. It may be more appropriate to look for adaptation to a native speaker language style. In this respect, examination boards may be drawing the wrong conclusions and misleading examiners. This is a matter which needs further investigation.

References

Beebe, L. and H. Giles. 1989. 'Speech accommodation theories: discussions in terms of second language acquisition'. *International Journal for the Sociology of Language* 46, 5–32.

Bell, A. 1984. 'Language style as audience design'. *Language in Society* 13, 145–205.

Labov, W. 1972. 'Notes on linguistic methodology'. *Language in Society* 1, 97–120.

Laufer, B. and Nation ISP. 1995. 'Vocabulary size and use: lexical richness in L2 written production'. *Applied Linguistics* 16/3, 307–322.

Milroy, L. 1987. *Language and social networks*. Oxford: Basil Blackwell.

Appendix

Prompt sheet given to student pairs to generate discussion:

Your Country / My Country

Question your partner / group members closely to find out the following information about their country.
Make notes in case you are asked to report back at the end of the lesson.
Find out as much detail as you can.

Ask about:

1. the population of their country
2. the climate
3. the geography
4. the main religion
5. the political system
6. the economy
7. the main problems
8. the national characteristics of the people (physical and temperamental)
9. the role of the sexes in the family, in the workplace and in society

Try to find out the general attitude of people from your partner's country to:

a) Britain
b) your own country
c) America
d) other world super-powers

ALAN TONKYN AND JULIET WILSON
Revising the IELTS speaking test

Introduction: continuity vs. updating

In this paper we describe the process of revising the International English Language Testing Service (IELTS) speaking sub-test, a process that began in early 1998, and culminated in the introduction of the new test in July 2001.

When one is talking about a test revision project, the obvious starting point is the old test. If that test is a prestigious 'gatekeeping' proficiency test, the test updater faces the need to balance the need for continuity with the need for revision.

Given this demand for continuity, the test reviser must therefore face the 'if it ain't broke, don't fix it' argument. Why did the IELTS oral test seem in need of a measure of 'fixing'?

Reasons for updating: scale and tasks

The aspects of the test needing revision were of two kinds: the rating scale and the test tasks.

The old rating scale, last revised 11 years ago, was a nine-band holistic one, with band descriptions providing 'snapshots' of performance at each level. Although the descriptions given at each level seemed broadly appropriate and in line with the overall band descriptions published by the University of Cambridge Local Examinations Syndicate (UCLES), they were felt to need improvement in two respects:

a)   Like most rating scales of their period, they had not been systematically checked against the facts of real performances.
b)   The holistic 'snapshot' approach to describing levels raises another problem. The profile-writer may decide to put into each level profile only those features which are felt to be key distinguishing marks of that level. In the old IELTS scale this led to the disappearance from view of certain features in certain parts of the scale. Thus there were no overt mentions of pronunciation in bands 5, 6, and 7, or of fluency features in bands 6, 7, and 8.

If we turn now from the scale to the test tasks, the problem in the old test can be said to be a failure of development during the test interview. The test was designed in five phases, with phases 2–4 designed to push the candidate progressively to his/her linguistic 'ceiling'. However, it was found that phases 3 and 4, in which the candidate was required to elicit information, to express precise meaning and attitudes, and to speculate, did not always elicit a 'richer' performance. Moreover, these elicitation problems led, in turn, to variations in amounts and type of examiner-talk.

Key principles guiding our revisions

Three main principles guided our work:

Theoretical relevance: The test's criteria and tasks should be defensible in terms of valid theories of oral performance.

Discriminating power: The test criteria and tasks should enable relevant distinctions to be made between candidates.

Assessability: The features selected for assessor attention should be salient enough for a single interviewer-assessor to notice them.

With these principles in mind, we now turn to some of the influences on the revised speaking test.

Theoretical background: higher and lower proficiency

Let us start with theoretical relevance, and a general statement.

Current cognitive views of the speech production process (e.g., Levelt, 1989; Garman, 1990) suggest the proficient L2 speaker will possess the following:

a) a wide *repertoire* of lexis and grammar to enable flexible, appropriate, precise construction of utterances in 'real time' (the knowledge factor);

b) a set of established *procedures* for pronunciation and lexico-grammar, and a set of established 'chunks' of language, all of which will enable fluent performance with 'on-line' planning reduced to acceptable amounts and timing (the processing factor).

Research suggests the following features are characteristic of more and less proficient oral performances (e.g., Albrechtsen et al., 1980; Butcher, 1980; Freed, 1995; Fulcher, 1996; Lazaraton, 1998; Lennon, 1990, 1995; Pennington, 1992; Raupach, 1980; Riggenbach, 1991; Temple, 2000; Towell et al., 1996; Van Gelderen, 1994).

Less proficient	*More proficient*
Shorter and less complex 'units' of speech	Longer and more complex (e.g., more embedded) units of speech
More errors per unit of speech	Fewer errors per unit of speech
Less, and more limited, use of cohesive markers	More, and more varied, use of cohesive markers
Lexis: Use of common words	Lexis: use of more sophisticated and idiomatic vocabulary
Pauses linked to language search	Pauses linked to content search
Pauses within grammatical constituents	Pauses between grammatical constituents
More silent pause time	Less silent pause time
Shorter 'runs' of speech between noticeable pauses	Longer runs of speech between noticeable pauses
Speed of delivery noticeably below native speaker rate	Speed of delivery not noticeably below native speaker rate

We have so far set out what we would see as the main theoretically relevant and helpfully discriminating features of spoken language which assessors might look for. In addition, one can mention some other factors which oral test designers need to be aware of. Firstly, research (Fulcher, 1993; Lazaraton, 1998) has suggested that particular errors may be difficult to associate with particular levels or with intelligibility problems. Secondly, Taylor and Jones have found, in analyses of pilot versions of the new speaking test, that pronunciation seems to attract distinctive ratings from assessors (2001). Finally, Tonkyn's 1999 analysis of the nature of IELTS-rated oral performances found there may be complex and variable interactions of features (e.g., fluency with complexity and/or accuracy) to produce an overall rating.

Assessability problems

Let us now mention some assessability issues which other studies have thrown up.

Pollitt and Murray, examining the features attended to by raters, have noted that the relative importance of certain traits will be affected by the speaker's proficiency level (1996). Thus, at lower levels, grammatical features seem to be key determinants of the score awarded, whereas higher up there is more attention to discoursal features. Hence, though a user-friendly scale should probably describe features such as accuracy throughout the scale, it should also be sensitive to necessary changes of focus at different levels.

A small-scale study by Tonkyn (1992) in which nine raters noted the features which contributed to their rating decisions while assessing six taped interviews, produced the following 'top five' rank order in terms of number of mentions:

1. Pronunciation (43 mentions)
2. Fluency (31)
3. Grammatical accuracy (27)
4. Vocabulary (22)
5. Communication of information (20)

These expressed preferences suggest that the more linguistic features seem to be the most salient to raters 'on the job'.

Scale revision: holistic or analytical?

The existing scale, as mentioned before, was a holistic one, with a single description at each level. The revision committee felt that an analytical scale, with separate assessments of a number of performance features, would have certain advantages:

a)   It would allow for more consistent and visible treatment of features throughout the scale.
b)   It would permit some recognition of the complex and variable ways in which features can interact to build up an overall performance profile.
c)   It would help, as Hughes has argued (1989), to improve the reliability of ratings, requiring a number of potentially independent judgements of a performance rather than just one.

Scale revision: features selected

A four-parameter scale has been developed which we feel will not be over-burdensome, and will provide a coherent set of sub-scales with few overlaps:

- Fluency and coherence
- Lexical resource
- Grammatical range and accuracy
- Pronunciation

Clear operationalisation of terms used in a scale is important. Here is an example, in abbreviated form, of the ways in which these parameters are defined for the examiners:

Lexical resource

This refers to the range of vocabulary at the candidate's disposal, which will influence the range of topics which he/she can discuss, and the precision with which meanings are expressed and attitudes conveyed. Indicators will be:

- variety of words used;
- adequacy and appropriacy of vocabulary in relation to the requirements of referential meaning (correct labelling), style, collocation/idiom, expression of attitude to content; and
- ability to use paraphrase.

The production of the rating scales themselves was a to-and-fro process of gradual refinement, drawing on the results of research and on the experience of a number of existing IELTS examiners.

The scale descriptions

The new scales mention, *inter alia*, the following features:

- the position and function (i.e., content- or language-focused) of hesitations;
- the use of connectives and other cohesive features;
- distinctions between idiomatic/sophisticated vocabulary, and the ability to paraphrase;
- the ability to produce complex sentence forms, especially sub-ordinate clauses, and to mix simple and complex structures; and
- the relationships between complexity and fluency and between complexity and accuracy.

In addition, pronunciation is defined at only four levels (bands 2, 4, 6, and 8): it is felt that nine-level distinctions would be unrealistic.

Overall, we feel this scale is truer to the facts of oral performance and allows more consistent treatment of relatively salient, assessable features.

The format of the revised IELTS speaking test

The revised test is divided into three main parts. Each part fulfils a specific function in terms of interaction pattern, task input, and candidate output.

In Part 1 (4–5 minutes), candidates answer general questions about themselves, their homes/families, their jobs/studies, their interests, and a range of similar topic areas. In Part 2, (3–4 minutes), candidates are given a prompt and asked to talk on a particular topic for one or two minutes after one minute's preparation time. In Part 3 (4–5 minutes), examiner and candidate engage in a discussion of more general or abstract issues which are thematically linked to the topic in Part 2.

The test has been designed so there is a progression from familiar topics to more unfamiliar ones – a move from less to more challenging subject matters. However, candidates will now be assessed on a sustained performance over the three parts of the speaking test: they are no longer seen as moving towards a 'linguistic ceiling' as the test proceeds.

The long turn in Part 2, which provides candidates with an opportunity for sustained language production and for taking the initiative in the interaction, is a particular and distinct enhancement to the current test.

Research (e.g., Wigglesworth, 1997; Skehan and Foster, 1997) indicates preparation time enhances performance, so this has been included for the new Part 2. Candidates' prompt cards for Part 2 assist them by providing contexts and content points to guide them through their long turns. Again, these do not need to be followed strictly, but they provide support for weaker candidates. This is an example of what a candidate might receive:

Describe a teacher or lecturer who has influenced you in your education.

You should say:

where you met them
what subject they taught
what was special about them

and explain why this person influenced you so much.

The prolonged turn also gives the examiner, freed from interviewing, the time to focus entirely on the performance. This is an important factor in improving the reliability and accuracy of the assessment.

If candidates produce a memorised speech in Part 2, examiners are instructed to base their rating on Parts 1 and 3 of the test, using the questions in Part 3 to check on the candidate's understanding of topics dealt with in Part 2.

The format of the new test has been designed to suit both Academic and General Training candidates. Part 1 deals with topics familiar to all those taking the test. Part 2 requires seminar-type presentation skills, but uses topics accessible to all. Part 3 invites the less competent speakers to explain and describe while those at a higher linguistic level can develop arguments, justify opinions, analyse, and speculate.

A significant change in the test procedures concerns the use of the Examiner Frame. This is a script for the examiner's role in the conversation with the candidate, guiding the management of the test at each stage. The wording in the frame is carefully controlled in Parts 1 and 2 to ensure that all candidates receive the same input, delivered in the same manner. This is an example of a Part 1 frame:

Frame 1 Home town/village

Let's talk about your home town or village...

What kind of place is it?
What's the most interesting part of your town/village?
What kind of jobs do people in your town/village do?
Would you say it is a good place to live? [Why?]

In Part 1, examiners must not deviate from the frame. In Part 2, they are allowed to clarify a word briefly and to repeat, but not to rephrase, the prompt. In Part 3, the two-way discussion, the frame is looser and examiners can accommodate their language to the level of the candidate by fashioning appropriate questions from graded prompts. The frame also provides support for lower level candidates while still allowing higher level candidates to demonstrate their proficiency.

The trialling that has been carried out in the UK and Australia indicates candidates have reacted positively to this new format. Individual comments have praised such things as the 'broader range of topics' (seen as more challenging), and the usefulness of the long turn. Interestingly, one candidate noted approvingly that the new test is 'more formal, more like a real test', whilst another reported that he felt 'more comfortable' with the new format. The comment on the broader range of the new test is supported by Lazaraton's study of speaking functions elicited by the trial test versions (2000).

These are the functions that Lazaraton identified as emerging regularly although there obviously will be others that will occur but are not forced by the test structure:

- Providing personal information
- Providing non-personal information
- Expressing opinions
- Explaining
- Suggesting
- Justifying opinions
- Speculating

- Expressing a preference
- Comparing and contrasting
- Summarising
- Conversation repair
- Narrating and paraphrasing
- Analysing
- Qualifying

In conclusion, the tasks in the IELTS speaking test have been designed with a bias for best for examiners, who now have a more user-friendly and standardised brief, and for candidates who will have more opportunity to speak at length and display the full range of their ability in English.

References

Albrechtsen, D., B. Henrikson, and C. Faerch. 1980. 'Native speaker reactions to learners' spoken interlanguage'. *Language Learning* 30, 365–396.

Butcher, A. 1980. 'Pause and syntactic structure'. In H. Dechert and M. Raupach (eds.) *Temporal Variables in Speech: Studies on Honour of Frieda Goldman-Eisler.* The Hague: Mouton, 85–90.

Freed, B. 1995. 'What makes us think that students who study abroad become fluent?' In B. Freed (ed.) *Second Language Acquisition in a Study Abroad Context.* Amsterdam: John Benjamins, 123–148.

Fulcher, G. 1993. 'The construction and validation of rating scales for oral tests in English as a foreign language'. Unpublished PhD thesis: University of Lancaster.

Fulcher, G. 1996. 'Does thick description lead to smart tests? A data-based approach to rating scale construction'. *Language Testing* 13/2, 208–238.

Garman, M. 1990. *Psycholinguistics.* Cambridge: Cambridge University Press.

Hughes, A. 1989. *Testing for Language Teachers*. Cambridge: Cambridge University Press.

Lazaraton, A. 1998. 'An analysis of differences in linguistic features of candidates at different levels of the IELTS speaking test'. UCLES EFL: Unpublished internal report.

Lazaraton, A. 2000. 'An analysis of the relationship between task features and candidate output for the revised speaking test'. UCLES EFL: Unpublished internal report.

Lennon, P. 1990 'Investigating fluency in EFL: a quantitative approach'. *Language Learning* 40, 387–417.

Lennon, P. 1995. 'Assessing short-term change in advanced oral proficiency: problems of reliability and validity in four case studies'. *ITL Review of Applied Linguistics*, 75–110.

Levelt, W. 1989. *Speaking: from Intention to Articulation*. Cambridge, Mass.: MIT Press.

Pennington, M.C. 1992. 'Discourse factors related to L2 phonological proficiency: an exploratory study'. *Perspectives* 4/2, 25–39.

Pollitt, A. and N. Murray. 1996. 'What raters *really* pay attention to'. In M. Milanovic and N. Saville (eds.) *Studies in Language Testing: 3*. Cambridge: Cambridge University Press, 74–91.

Raupach, M. 1980. 'Temporal variables in first and second language speech production'. In H. Dechert and M. Raupach (eds.) *Temporal Variables in Speech: Studies on Honour of Frieda Goldman-Eisler*. The Hague: Mouton, 263–270.

Riggenbach, H. 1991. 'Toward an understanding of fluency: a micro-analysis of nonnative speaker conversations'. *Discourse Processes* 14, 423–441.

Skehan, P. and P. Foster. 1997. 'The influence of planning and post-task activities on accuracy and complexity in task-based learning'. *Language Teaching Research* 1/3, 185–211.

Taylor, L. and N. Jones. 2001. 'Revising the IELTS speaking test'. *Research Notes* 4, 9–12. (UCLES)

Temple, L. 2000. 'Second language learner speech production'. *Studia Linguistica* 54/2, 288–297.

Tonkyn, A. 1992. 'Testing oral language as behaviour: problems and principles in the use of proficiency rating scales'. In S. Rama Devi, R. Mathew, R. Eapen, K. Kumar, and J. Tharu (eds.) *The ELT Curriculum: Emerging Issues*. Delhi: BP Pub. corp., 139– 160

Tonkyn, A. 1999. 'Reading University / UCLES IELTS Rating Research Project – Interim Report'. UCLES EFL: Unpublished internal report.

Towell, R., R. Hawkins, and N. Bazergui. 1996. 'The development of fluency in advanced learners of French'. *Applied Linguistics* 17/1, 84–119.

Van Gelderen, A. 1994. 'Prediction of global ratings of fluency and delivery in narrative discourse by linguistic and phonetic measures – oral performances of students aged 11–12 years'. *Language Testing* 11/3, 291–319.

Wigglesworth, G. 1997. 'An investigation of planning time and proficiency level on oral test discourse'. *Language Testing* 14/1, 101–122.

Section 6:
Research and Publication

JO MCDONOUGH
Patterns of change in EAP research methodology

Introduction

The aim of this paper is to examine the main trends in English for Academic Purposes (EAP) research methodology, and the relationship between methods on the one hand and content/focus on the other. The paper argues there is evidence of imbalance in methods choice which may reflect under-explored areas of EAP research activity, even a paradigm gap, and that this imbalance points to some possible directions for future research.

The data set on which this analysis is based comprises published British Association of Lecturers in English for Academic Purposes (BALEAP) conference proceedings 1975–1995.[1] (A list of all titles is in the appendix). The justification for this is partly that the data set is manageable, but also that the biennial conference represents a major aspect of the public face of UK EAP. A further significant point here is that language teachers in higher education – BALEAP practitioners among them – are often by the nature of their jobs 'academics', but at the same time teach on the summer pre-sessional course and the late afternoon in-sessional programme. In other words, they are in an interesting position on a putative 'theory-practice' spectrum and in a unique position to engage in practice-driven research. Ur is one of a number of writers to speak of a boundary line distinguishing the 'academic' and the 'professional' (1992), and we return later to the question of where BALEAP-type practitioners are located on such a line.

---

1   The 1997 conference on testing and the 1999 one on technologies were rather specialised in theme and therefore would have considerably skewed the data.

The data

As a working definition I follow Nunan who characterises research as 'a systematic process of enquiry consisting of 3 elements [...] 1) a question, problem or hypothesis 2) data 3) analysis and interpretation of data' (1992). Further, for the present analysis I have taken a paper as 'research' if it fulfils these conditions: 1) that research methods are explicitly stated; 2) that the research forms a central part of the paper; and 3) that the research was carried out by the authors themselves.

Overall the breakdown is as follows:

No. of publications 1975–1995 = 11
No. of papers in total = 163
No. of research papers = 70, i.e., 43 per cent of total

The rank order of research methods used and their numerical frequency, taking mixed or multiple methods as one entity:

Language data/text analysis	25
Mixed (i.e. > method)	20
Questionnaire	16
Interview	4
Test data	3
Observation	2

The rank order separating out multiple methods:

Questionnaire	31
Language data/text analysis	28
Interview	20
Observation (incl. tapes)	8
Test data	4
Documents (e.g., course handouts)	4
Diaries	1

The following table summarises these methods diachronically (brackets simply indicate that the method is referred to but is not primary):

Year	No/ with res	Qnnaire	Text/ lang	Intv	Obsvn	Test	Docs	Mixed	Case
1975	16/7	7	(1)						
1977	18/2		2		(1)				
1979	12/5		1	2		2		1	(1)
1981	14/4	1	2					1	(1)
1983	10/3		2					1	
1985	17/6	1	4					1	
1987	13/8	2	2	1		1		2	1
1989	9/7	1	1		1			3	1
1991	17/9	2	4					3	1
1993	20/10	1	3		1			5	2
1995	17/9	1	4	1				3	1

Analysis

The data lend themselves to a number of comments.

1. Questionnaires have been used steadily, with a preponderance in the 'early days' represented here. Since questionnaires are particularly associated with survey research, and the EAP focus is on such areas as needs analysis, language and student profiles, and course design, they have clearly played an important role in establishing key parameters for the whole field of EAP.
2. There has been a trend towards using two or more methods together, thus to an extent broadening the methodological base: the increase in the use of interviews in this context is particularly noticeable. Multiple methods occasionally result in explicit triangulation between data sources.
3. 'Text analysis' has become increasingly significant, and here includes language structure, discourse, corpora, and genre. Models of analysis have become less intuitive and more explicit. There is a clear focus on target-situation language data; in other words, this kind of analysis is by and large product-oriented, dealing in the discipline destinations for which students are headed. We return to this point below.
4. Case studies are not of course methods in themselves; in fact they often employ several methods in order to focus on the object of interest – text, learner, genre 'event' (such as dissertation), and so on. They are included here because as the table shows there are few of them overall, even fewer dealing with individual learners and teachers, and this itself is significant in terms of research orientation in the profile as a whole.
5. From a methods perspective, some aspects are markedly under-represented. First of all, and rather curiously, the 1983 conference title notwithstanding, the EAP classroom receives much less attention in its own right as a locus of teaching and learning than as a reflection of target-situation concerns and data and the context of the disciplines (materials/syllabus design based on target needs, team teaching, for example). To borrow Freeman's

phrase, what most papers are concerned with is the 'epistemo-logy of the product' rather than the process of teaching (2000). Secondly, there are few or no instances of such research tools as observation, diaries, narratives, think-aloud protocols, and other forms of introspection (and indeed interviews only appear much in company with other methods). Thirdly, there is little that is genuinely small-scale (except in some of the micro-studies of specific genres), as can be seen from the limited number of case studies. Where research *is* perceived to be small-scale, this is often presented rather apologetically, for instance:

This is only experimental

Hard information (referring to statistics, percentages, averages)

Only a small piece of research

This paper is anecdotal

This is only a small-scale study

This is only speculative

There is no claim to typicality

This was intuitively felt

This draws only upon experience

Based only on subjective impressions

These results are taken from a very small corpus of data and I would not wish to read too much into them

and so on. There is an implication here of a hidden agenda which regards the potential generalisability of research outcomes as a desideratum and takes a more cautious view of the particular instance and the experiential.

Discussion

I would claim from this brief analysis that, although most of this research can certainly be described as 'applied' rather than theoretical, or normative, there is in the data a dominant paradigm that leaves a major research tradition underrepresented, namely the qualitative/

interpretive/naturalistic approach. This kind of approach manifests itself in a number of ways. For instance, data are often collected first as a way of generating research questions; such data tend to be 'thick' and text-rich (narratives, diaries, descriptive observation, and so on); the individual case is positively sought out for itself rather than primarily as a representative instance of a larger set; the understanding of meanings in localised contexts is central; bias and subjectivity are therefore necessary criteria.

There are to be sure some clear exceptions to be found. Houghton presents a case study of Mr Chong (1987); Meldrum points towards action research as an appropriate paradigm (1993); Furneaux and colleagues describe a micro-ethnography (of target situation seminars) (1989); and Thorp and Harris offer the most explicit methodological framework, including a data-first approach, an ethnographic perspective, a justification of subjectivity, and a recognition of the need to discuss such 'technical' issues as validity, reliability, and triangulation in interpretive research (1993).[2]

This is in no way to argue ourselves into the facile position that quantification is inherently 'wrong', and a research stance should necessarily entail openness to all methods as the basis for appropriate choice. Nevertheless, and particularly in view of current trends in both education and general English Language Teaching (ELT) (see, e.g., Hopkins, 1993; Wallace, 1991), it is surprising that such 'alternative' approaches and methods are so little in evidence in EAP. We can consider just a few suggestions as to how the focus of attention might shift with greater use of the kinds of underrepresented methods we have been discussing – and indeed vice versa, namely how a shift of focus towards the empirical data of the EAP classroom would entail a broader view of methods as well:

---

2   Outside of the current data set mention should also be made of James'
     benchmark case study of Marcos, and within genre/corpus analysis there are
     some interesting instances of use of informants via interviews, i.e., broadening
     the discourse community notion in texts to encompass the views of actual
     participants. See for example Swales et al. (1999) and Hyland (2001).

- Case studies of individual learners
- Case studies of individual teachers
- Action research projects for change and innovation
- Teachers' planning strategies and how they relate to course specifications
- Learners' differing uses of classroom resources
- Teachers' attitudes to target disciplines and beliefs about language and specialism
- Uptake of target-related training by learners: where does the EAP teaching 'go'?
- The role and nature of teachers' classroom decisions
- What is 'special' about the EAP classroom as evidenced from classroom data?
- How do teachers adapt EAP teaching materials?

Much could undoubtedly be added to this list (and see, e.g., Bailey and Nunan (1996) as a rich source of ideas from general ELT).

There is one further important issue. In the current climate in UK universities, 'research' is to a large extent associated with winning research grants, with contractual obligations and expectations, and crucially with funding (the Research Assessment Exercise – the RAE – periodically being by far the major preoccupation of most if not all university departments). Many EAP staff members are affected by these considerations, it has to be said, negatively as well as positively. However, for many EAP professionals who are not required to be involved in this way, 'research' may not be seen to be part of their brief. Indeed it is sometimes actively discouraged in a sharp separation between teaching and research, so there is no expectation of research output and no time allocated to it either. Therefore, the professional is not a unitary one, and there is a sense that practitioners may be on one side or the other of the kind of dividing line postulated by Ur (see above). In such a setting teachers – be they regular staff, pre-session tutors, and so on – are often 'walled out', in Freeman's terms (2000) and their voices not heard, because research is not a routine part of their everyday professional lives and because the dominant paradigm and its associated methods do not tap into the complex reality of their experiential contexts. Erickson, in a key paper on qualitative method, makes the point that everyday life is often 'invisible' precisely because it is familiar, so in order to reflect on it and analyse it, it is necessary to 'make the familiar strange' (1986). I would argue that in EAP, we have spent a good deal of time and energy very productively and necessarily establishing the field by researching target situations and discipline contexts, in other words 'making the strange familiar'. It is now time to shift our attention to the local familiarity of the EAP classroom and to look at the complexities of that as a context in its own right.

To a considerable degree BALEAP has been a key player in establishing the discipline of EAP, and is well placed to push against and extend the current research boundaries in new directions. Although Hyland was referring to texts, we might borrow a perspective from him and apply it to research methods, arguing that they are not simply a value-free bank of possibilities, but that they '[...] offer a window on the practices and beliefs of the communities for which they have meaning' (2000).

References

Bailey, K. and D. Nunan (eds.). 1996. *Voices from the Language Classroom*. Cambridge: Cambridge University Press

Erickson, F. 1986. 'Qualitative methods in research on teaching'. In M. Wittrock (ed.) *A Handbook of Research on Teaching*. NY: Macmillan, 119–161.

Freeman, D. 2000. 'Practical epistemologies: mapping the boundaries of teachers' work'. *Proceedings of IATEFL Conference 2000*, 10–21.

Hopkins, D. 1993. *A Teacher's Guide to Classroom Research*. Buckingham and Philadelphia: Open University Press.

Hyland, K. 2000. *Disciplinary Discourses: Social Interaction in Academic Writing*. Harlow: Pearson Education/Longman.

Hyland, K. 2001. 'Humble servants of the discipline? Self-mention in research articles'. *English for Specific Purposes* 20/3, 207–226.

Nunan, D. 1992. *Research Methods in Language Learning*. Cambridge: Cambridge University Press.

Swales, J., U. Ahmad, Y-Y. Chang, D. Chavez, D. Dressen, and R. Seymour. 1998. 'Consider this: the role of imperatives in scholarly writing'. *Applied Linguistics* 19/1, 97–121.

Ur, P. 1992. 'Teacher learning'. *ELT Journal* 46/1, 56–61.

Wallace, M. 1991. *Training Foreign Language Teachers: A Reflective Approach*. Cambridge: Cambridge University Press.

Appendix

Publications used (chronological):

1975   English for Academic Purposes
        Papers on the language problems of overseas students in
        higher education in the UK

1977   Pre-sessional courses for overseas students

1979   Study modes and academic development of overseas students

1981   The ESP teacher: role, development, and prospects

1983   The ESP classroom

1985   Academic writing: process and product

1987   Autonomy and individualisation in language learning

1989   Socio-cultural issues in English for Academic Purposes

1991   Language, learning and success: studying through English

1993   Evaluation and course design in EAP

1995   Academic standards and expectations: the role of EAP

KEITH MORROW
Getting published in an academic journal

This is an essentially practical paper looking at the process of getting published in an academic journal, and passing on some advice from the author's perspective as a journal editor.

For some members of BALEAP, writing articles for journals may seem like something that other people do. Journals are there to be read, reviewed, or critiqued, but not to be written for. After all, who would be interested in what I have done, what I have found out, or what I have thought? And is it worth my time anyway to sit down and write an article? I've heard you don't even get paid for it.

Of course the answer to all these rhetorical questions is as obvious as the answer to rhetorical questions usually is: *it all depends*. Clearly nobody will be interested in what you have done, found out, or thought just because you are the one who has done it, found it out, or thought it. And clearly nobody ever got rich by writing journal articles. But I want to suggest a number of reasons why you might seriously consider making writing for a journal a part of your professional development, and then look at some practical tips on how to do it.

How to recognise a journal

First, though, the question of definition. What is a journal? It is difficult to pin down, since journals come in a variety of guises, but like the snark, you usually recognise one when you see it. Typically a journal is a collection of articles (What is an article? We'll come back to that) and other types of text (e.g., book reviews, correspondence, special features of different kinds) in a particular professional/academic area, published at regular intervals (often quarterly). There are many international journals in the field of ELT/TEFL and some of the best known would be *Applied Linguistics, ELT Journal, TESOL Quarterly*, and *ESP Journal*; in addition there are many more local journals, circulating primarily in a particular country or region. Examples of these would be *The ACELT Journal* (Philippines), *JALT Journal* (Japan), and *NovELTy* (Hungary). There is a very useful collection of journal details from all round the world on http://www.tesol.org/pubs/author/books/demystify.html. These journals are all different in the audiences they cater to, and in the type of articles they publish. But there is one true test to see whether a publication is a journal or something else.

In a journal, decisions about whether an article should be published or not are not made by the editor alone. All journals operate a policy of peer review, under which submissions are considered by fellow professionals to evaluate their interest and value in terms of possible publication; in most cases the review is 'blind' with the submission being considered in an anonymous form, so recommendations about publication or non-publication are not influenced by preconceptions based on knowledge of its authorship. I will look further at the mechanics of this process later, but for the moment it is the principle that is important. A policy of blind peer review means that any article accepted for publication has been recognised as having value by representatives of the profession; it means that a reader is entitled to take what it says seriously (if critically); and it means that the writer is entitled to feel that she/he is making a valid professional contribution through what has been written.

This is not to deny the value and possible interest of publications containing writing on professional topics which has not been the subject of peer review. In our field, *English Teaching Professional, Modern English Teacher*, and *The Teacher Trainer* are examples of publications where decisions about publication are essentially in the hands of the editors, aided by whatever advice they choose to take to back up their own professional judgement. The quality and interest of what is published is precisely a function of this professional judgment, and in the case of these three examples, it is usually very high. But publications without peer review are not journals; they are something else.

In some cases, it can be very important whether you publish in a peer-reviewed journal or in a non peer-reviewed magazine or newsletter. The most obvious example is if you are working in an academic institution, or trying to make an academic reputation for yourself. These days many universities expect their staff to publish work in recognised journals, and decisions about appointment, promotion, and tenure are often based on the publications record of the individual concerned. In this case, it is only work published in peer-reviewed journals which counts.

Reasons to write

One very good reason for writing for publication has already been mentioned. It can help you to get, and keep a job. But there are other reasons, which apply equally to people working in academic contexts where publication is expected, and in other fields, where it is not the norm. I would suggest these reasons can be divided into two sets, each connected to one of the possible interpretations of the ambiguous phrase 'professional development'.

The first set has to do with its interpretation in the sense of the development of you, personally, as a professional. Writing for professional colleagues about what you have done, found out, or thought involves making these things explicit, and often it is only when you begin to make them explicit for other people that you make them explicit for yourself. In other words, the act of writing about something can often help you to understand it better – this of course is what lies behind the idea of journal writing in its other sense, that of writing reflections on our experiences to help us to learn from them. But writing for an external audience is rather different from writing for ourselves. It requires explicitness about rationale and procedure, so that readers can be absolutely sure why you say what you say, or why you did what you did; and it requires you to situate what you write in a broader professional context, so that readers can see easily how your work relates to that of others in a similar field. Both of these requirements are ones which can be invaluable for you personally. Laying bare the hidden assumptions behind your work will always be difficult and it may sometimes be uncomfortable, but it can be extremely productive; and going outside the immediate context in which you are working to see what you can learn from the work of others is a key aspect of the ongoing development of you as a professional.

The other meaning of professional development is, of course, the development of the profession. It is important not to get swept up in pious platitudes, or to exaggerate the importance and impact of any individual's contribution, but in a very real sense the status of EAP as a profession depends on the existence of a shared body of knowledge and skills, insight and experience. EAP professionals do not exist in a vacuum, but can draw on the work of professional colleagues. But if we are serious as professionals, it is not unreasonable to argue that we have a responsibility to contribute to the development of our profession, not just to use the work of others. Napoleon apparently revealed his megalomaniac tendencies through the phrase 'L'empire, c'est moi' – the empire is me. It is anything but megalomaniacal to suggest that in a very real sense, the profession is us.

Steps to writing for publication

Step 1: Who are you writing for?

The very first step in deciding to write an article is to decide who to write it for. Please, never ever sit down to write an article. Instead, sit down to write an article for *ESP Journal* or for *Modern English Teacher*. One of the commonest and most frustrating mistakes writers make is to produce a piece of work, and only then think about where they want to try to publish it. All over the world, editors of journals and newsletters are bombarded with material which is manifestly unsuitable in terms of topic and treatment for their particular publication, but which authors have submitted, apparently without doing the most basic homework about their intended target. Journals are not interchangeable, and an article which is to have a chance of publication must be written with its intended audience very much in mind.

This means that as a potential contributor, you need to do some research. If you want to submit to *ELT Journal*, to *TESOL Quarterly*, or any other journal, then get hold of some back copies. Look through the topics, look at the way articles treat themes, look at the conventions of form and presentation; get hold of the contributors' guidelines to get information about length, layout, and referencing. You will see that there is usually an implicit model underlying most of the articles published in any given journal. Follow it.

Step 2: What are you going to write about?

The most obvious answer is that it must be something you know about, but *know about* is not a very satisfactory term. In education we are familiar with the distinction between declarative knowledge and procedural knowledge. In school and at university, declarative knowledge is often highly prized. Showing that you know *about* something is an important aspect of most work we do there, and this means that school and university work often has a display function, acting as a vehicle for us to demonstrate to our teachers what we know. This is categorically not the case with writing for publication.

One of the fundamentals of writing is that we write for an audience, and no real-world audience is interested in a mere display of what a writer knows about a particular area. Procedural knowledge, however, has a much wider appeal. If you can share with your reader ideas about *how* to do things, particularly if this is based on your own experience, and can be made relevant to theirs, then the chances are the audience will be interested.

There is one further point about choosing a topic for an article. Your theme needs to be rooted in your personal experience, but it also needs to be relevant to the readers of the journal, who in the case of international journals, may be on the other side of the world. This means that you have to strike a very careful balance between an over-detailed concern with parochial issues, and over-general 'waffle'. In fact one of the very hardest parts of writing an article for a general audience is deciding how to contextualise the work you are reporting in a way which will be relevant and interesting for your readers, and also how to help them to make connections between the specifics of your situation (which you know about) and the specifics of theirs (which you don't). The approach which is often recommended is to treat your piece of work as an exemplar, showing how it addresses general issues in a particular context, but highlighting the ways in which other contexts may require different solutions.

Step 3: How to deal with the topic

This is largely a matter of developing the ideas outlined above. Knowing which publication you are writing for and therefore who the likely audience will be allows you to make decisions about the best way to handle the topic you have chosen. But there are a number of key things to check as you go along, and certainly before you send your finished article off:

- Is it clear that the article is about something and that the points made all relate back to this 'something'?
- Have I presented it in the most interesting way?
- Am I telling the reader anything new?
- Is there an appropriate balance between theory and practice?
- Have I organised the text clearly to help the reader find her/his way through it?
- Have I met all the 'formal' requirements of the particular publication I am writing for? Length? Layout? References?

Of course these all seem obvious points. But the most obvious ones are the ones that as an author you are most likely to overlook. You can become so engrossed in the manuscript you are producing that the reality of the outside world (for whom you are actually producing your work) can become blurred. That is why it is important on a practical level to take time over writing, to leave it and come back to it, and when you have 'finished' it, to leave it to mature for at least a couple of days before you re-read it and think about sending it off.

From the point of view of an editor, the most dispiriting contributions to receive are those which do not meet one of the first three criteria above. Pages of text which do not seem to be going anywhere, and which turn out to be just a rehash of familiar ideas are a waste of everybody's time; even the most original or innovative piece of work can be spoilt through a write-up which does not engage the reader. The single most important piece of advice is implicit in this. As a writer, think about the reader.

Behind the scenes

One cardinal rule is that you do not submit the same piece to more than one publication at the same time. You will in any case have written your article with a particular publication in mind, but you should also remember that the process of dealing with submissions is quite a complex one for underpaid, or even unpaid, journal editors and if you waste their time by making them deal with material already under consideration elsewhere, you are likely to get a frosty reception in future.

So what happens to your article after you have sent it in to your chosen journal? In detail, this varies of course according to the particular publication you have submitted it to, but the following stages which articles submitted to *ELT Journal* pass through, are typical of what happens to submissions to a peer-reviewed journal.

| Article received and acknowledged |

⇩

| Batch of articles sent out to appropriate members of the editorial advisory panel. Each article sent to at least two members of the panel |

⇩

| Reviews of articles sent to editor by members of the editorial advisory panel |

⇩

| Editor considers reviews from panel and decides on appropriate action for each submission |

◁   ⇩   ◁

| Reject: author receives brief feedback explaining why article cannot be accepted | Request revision: author receives detailed feedback identifying changes needed before article can be considered further | Accept: author receives offer of publication, sometimes subject to minor amendments |

⇩

⇦ | Re-submitted article goes to panel for further consideration | ⇨

As can be seen, this is quite a complex process and it can take time. At *ELT Journal*, we aim to let contributors know within 10–12 weeks whether or not we can publish their submission, but sometimes this timescale is exceeded. It may happen, for example, that your submission arrives just after a batch of articles is sent out to the panel. The next batch will probably not go out for another four or five weeks so this is dead time for your piece. Equally, a particular member of the panel may be away, ill, or just overworked when your article arrives for review so despite the best efforts of the editor, there may be a delay before you hear back. The keynote is patience. Everybody knows how important it is for you, and everybody will do their best to deal with your article as professionally as they can.

The truth

At *ELT Journal*, we receive around 200 submissions every year; in our four issues per year, we can publish approximately 30 articles. So the sad truth is that we cannot publish the overwhelming majority of those we receive. This picture is replicated for most of the international peer-review journals in our field. Because of the pressure on academics to publish (or be damned), there is enormous competition on the relatively few outlets, and so realistically you must be prepared for disappointment along the way to publication.

But realistically, you can also afford to be positive. Being involved in an interesting field such as EAP, having completed a postgraduate degree in the field, and having read this, you already have a head start. You can also increase your chances of getting published by choosing carefully the publications you target. Finally, remember that if you want to see your name in print, there are more ways than by writing a peer-reviewed article. Most publications include other features, letters pages for example, and most editors are very keen to publish correspondence which follows up issues raised in previous articles. You may not get many points for it in a research assessment exercise, but having a letter published in a prestigious journal is a good way to put yourself on the map – for the world at large, and for your own self image. And your mum will be really impressed!

Good luck.

George M. Blue / James Milton / Jane Saville (eds.)

Assessing English for Academic Purposes

Oxford, Bern, Berlin, Bruxelles, Frankfurt/M., New York, Wien, 2000. 289 pp.
ISBN 3-906765-98-9 / US-ISBN 0-8204-5316-1 pb.
sFr. 76.– / €* 51.80 / €** 48.40 / £ 31.– / US-$ 47.95

* includes VAT – only valid for Germany and Austria   ** does not include VAT

A concern for quality and the growing number of international students have made the assessment of English for Academic Purposes a prime concern in British universities. By drawing on the expertise of BALEAP and many EAP specialists, this collection describes and critically evaluates current issues and debates in the field. An introduction provides an overview of the state of assessment in EAP and this is followed by sections which investigate in depth individual issues such as the validity of commonly used tests, the utility of computer test batteries and other non-traditional forms of assessment. Also addressed with original research data are the varying requirements of individual departments, students' views of assessment and self-assessment instruments. These issues are relevant beyond the individual circumstances of British universities and should inform good practice not only in the UK but anywhere where students receive part or all of their education in English as a second or foreign language.

Contents: George M. Blue / James Milton / Jane Saville: Introduction: Assessing English for Academic Purposes – J. Charles Alderson: Testing in EAP: Progress? Achievement? Proficiency? – John Morley: The Chaplen Test Revisited – Paul Fanning / Lynne Hale: Screening New Students with the UCLES Computer Adaptive Test – Esther Daborn / Moira Calderwood: Collaborative Assessment of Written Reports: Electrical Engineering and EFL – Joan Cutting: Written Errors of International Students and English Native Speaker Students – Julie Hartill: Assessing Postgraduates in the Real World – Rita Green: Life after the Pre-Sessional Course: How Students Fare in their Departments – Lynn Errey: Stacking the Decks: What does it take to Satisfy Academic Readers' Requirements? – Gill Meldrum: I Know I have to be Critical, but How? – Katie Gray: Assessment in EAP: Moving away from Traditional Models – Alicia Cresswell: The Role of Portfolios in the Assessment of Student Writing on an EAP Course – M. I. Freeman: A Self-Evaluation Instrument for the Measurement of Student Proficiency Levels – George M. Blue: Self-Assessment and Defining Learners' Needs – Barbara Atherton: Developing Accuracy in Academic Writing – R. R. Jordan: Is the Customer Sometimes Right? Students' Views of Assessment in EAP.

PETER LANG
Bern · Berlin · Bruxelles · Frankfurt/M. · New York · Oxford · Wien

Giuseppina Cortese / Philip Riley (eds.)

Domain-specific English

Textual Practices across Communities and Classrooms

Bern, Berlin, Bruxelles, Frankfurt/M., New York, Oxford, Wien, 2002. 420 pp.
Linguistic Insights. Studies in Language and Communication. Vol. 2
General Editor: Maurizio Gotti
ISBN 3-906768-98-8 / US-ISBN 0-8204-5884-8 pb.
sFr. 97.– / €* 66.90 / €** 62.50 / £ 40.– / US-$ 62.95

* includes VAT – only valid for Germany and Austria   ** does not include VAT

Domain-specific discourse in English forms a continuum across the academic, professional and technical genres of all areas of knowledge. This collection of papers by scholars working in a variety of disciplines, cultural and institutional contexts forms an analytical and methodological framework for the discussion of a wide range of writing-related issues, problems and practices. The diversity of topics and perspectives represented here – including corpus-based approaches, discourse analysis and contrastive rhetoric, teaching methodology and domain-specific literacy, criticalness, linguistic ascendancy and the emergence of scientific English, identity and social epistemology – attests to the vitality and variety of sociolinguistic research in this complex and rapidly developing field.

Contents: Giuseppina Cortese/Philip Riley: Introduction – Philip Riley: Epistemic Communities: The Social Knowledge System, Discourse and Identity – Maurizio Gotti: The Development of English as a Language for Specialized Purposes – Christer Laurén: The Conflict between National Languages and English as the Languages of Arts and Sciences – Christopher N. Candlin/Vijay K. Bhatia/Christian H. Jensen: Must the Worlds Collide? Professional and Academic Discourses in the Study and Practice of Law – Anna Mauranen: «A Good Question.» Expressing Evaluation in Academic Speech – Teppo Varttala: Hedging in Scientific Research Articles: A Cross-disciplinary Study – Donna R. Miller: Probing Ways of Meaning in 'Technocratic' Discourse – Stefania Nuccorini: The Role of Dictionaries in Non-native Academic Writing: A Case Study – Maria Luisa Carrió: The Use of Phrasal Verbs by Native and Non-native Writers in Technical Articles – Tatiana Fedoulenkova: Idioms in Business English: Ways to Cross-cultural Awareness – Paola Giunchi: Information or Misinformation? 'Translating' Medical Research Papers into Web-posted Accounts – Izaskun Elorza: Assessing Translation in Domain-specific Learning Environments: A Study of Textual Variation – Hilkka Stotesbury: A Study of Interpretation in Critical Writing – Joseba M. González: In Search of Synergy: Agents Involved and Their Contribution – Giuseppina Cortese: My 'Doxy' Is Not Your 'Doxy': Doing Corpus Linguistics as Collaborative Design.

PETER LANG
Bern · Berlin · Bruxelles · Frankfurt/M. · New York · Oxford · Wien

Michael Grenfell / Michael Kelly / Diana Jones

The European Language Teacher

Recent Trends and Future Developments in Teacher Education

Oxford, Bern, Berlin, Bruxelles, Frankfurt/M., New York, Wien, 2003.
279 pp., 6 tables
ISBN 3-03910-070-X / US-ISBN 0-8204-6886-X pb.
sFr. 71.– / €* 48.90 / €** 45.70 / £ 32.– / US-$ 45.95
* includes VAT – only valid for Germany and Austria   ** does not include VAT

This book presents the European language teacher of tomorrow. It deals with recent trends and future developments in the training of second language teachers in Europe. Based on an EU-commissioned study of thirty-two countries, the book sets out the current provision of language teacher training across the age phases. Both pre-service and in-service teacher training is covered. Fifteen case studies of innovation and good practice are also presented. This detail is used to provide a needs analysis of training, on the basis of which a series of policy-orientated recommendations is developed. Finally, a professional profile of the European language teacher is constructed which lists the likely range of training and experience of tomorrow's teachers. These features are described in terms of *organisation*, *content* and *structure*. The book is framed by coverage of the contextual background to the study, both in terms of national priorities and EU policies, and a theoretical consideration of the issues in language teacher training.

Contents: Contexts for Teacher Training (The Social and Policy Context; Theories of Teacher Training) – Summary of Current Provision (Conditions and In-Service Training for Primary and Secondary Education) – Fifteen Case Studies of Good Practice – Furthering Good Practice (Needs Analysis, Recommendations, Professional Profile).

The Authors: Michael Grenfell is a Reader in Language in Education and Director of Research at the Graduate School of Education at the University of Southampton.

Michael Kelly is Professor of French at the University of Southampton and Director of the UK Subject Centre for Languages, Linguistics and Area Studies.

Diana Jones is a Research Assistant in the School of Modern Languages at the University of Southampton.

PETER LANG
Bern · Berlin · Bruxelles · Frankfurt/M. · New York · Oxford · Wien

KING ALFRED'S COLLEGE
LIBRARY